Two Minute Meditations....

A Daily Walk with the Saints

Mary A. Lombardo

JMJ Press

Albuquerque, New Mexico

JMJ Press
Albuquerque, New Mexico

Cover Artist: Jinger Heaston

All rights reserved

Copyright © 2009 by Mary A. Lombardo
ISBN: 978-1-933582-50-4

Published In the United States Of America

November 2009

Dedication

This book is dedicated to my family and friends who help
make my life's journey joyful.

INTRODUCTION

We are not alone on our journey through this life. We are part of the Communion of Saints.

The Communion of Saints is made up of three groups: those who are alive on earth, the Church Militant, that's us; the souls being purified in Purgatory to prepare for their acceptance into heaven, the Church Penitent; and the souls who have already joined God in Heaven, the Church Triumphant. St Paul writes about how we are all joined together in his letter to the Ephesians, 2:9. "Therefore, you are now no longer strangers and foreigners, but you are citizens with the saints and members of God's household."

What does this really mean for you and me? It means that we have a powerful support system that we

1

can call on in times of trouble. Not only can we ask the saints on earth, our friends and family, to pray for us, we can ask the saints in Purgatory as well as the saints who have joined God in Heaven. Think of the thousands and thousands of saints waiting to share our burdens and convey our needs to God. We have only to ask!

As saints ourselves, we can pray for our fellow saints on earth and for those who have passed from this life but have not yet come face-to-face with God.

When we pray to the saints in Heaven, we do not worship them. We show respect to all saints whether they have reached Heaven's door or are still struggling to reach that goal. We pay particular homage to the heavenly saints when we study their lives to learn which attributes give glory to God, and we try to imitate those virtues. Their lives are like a map to help us on our way. Through them we learn what it means to be courageous, unselfish, forgiving, charitable, loving, humble, and all the other wonderful characteristics their lives demonstrate.

In St. Paul's letter to the Hebrews, 6:11-12, he says, "But we want every one of you to show to the very end the same earnestness for the fulfillment of your hopes so that you may become not sluggish but imitators of those who by faith and patience will inherit the promises."

When we study the lives of the saints and begin to imitate them, we realize that the road to Heaven is not always easy, but, with the help of God and our fellow saints, we can reach our goal.

How will this book help you know and imitate the saints? Here's an opportunity to meet some saints who are new to you and to reacquaint yourself with some very familiar ones. For every day of the year, there is a short anecdote about a saint that illustrates a particular attribute that is pleasing to God and a prayer or meditation to help you imitate that virtue. Granted, you will most likely never have to show courage when facing wild animals in the Roman arena as many of our early martyrs did, but you can show courage by correcting someone who has a mistaken idea about your faith or who is straying from following God's word. Nor do you have to live like a hermit in a cave spending all your days meditating and praying like St. Antony of Egypt, but you can take time each day to think about God and perhaps read some scripture to gain new understanding about who He is and what He means in your life.

Learning about the saints helps us realize that we can imitate them in our own way and in our own time, so that we can become one of the Church Triumphant, one of the many saints who are privileged to be with God in Heaven for eternity.

If you look on any church calendar, you will find saints mentioned on many days of the year, but not all, as the Church does not assign a saint for each day. There are, however, many saints, mostly martyrs, who are recognized by the Church for each day of the year. Different dioceses can choose to honor other saints on days not set aside by the Church for specific saints. This is what I have done for this compilation of biographical anecdotes and meditations.

Sometimes not much is known about the early saints, so some of the included anecdotes may be based on legends that grew about each saint, but it makes sense that the legends were based on a strong characteristic of the saint and how he or she exhibited that strength throughout life.

You may have never heard of some of the saints that are mentioned in this book, but you will be inspired by the steadfastness they showed in their devotion to God. Their lives have so much to teach us about being responsible servants of Our Lord and Father.

+ January Opening Prayer +

Holy Saints, whom we remember this month of January, help me to read the stories of your lives with understanding of what it cost you to follow God's word. Open my heart that I may imitate you in any way I can for the glory of God. *"Sing to the Lord a new song; sing to the Lord, all lands." Psalm 95:1*

January 1 St. Telemachus (d. 404) was a Christian monk in a dark period of history when crowds of Romans cheered as Christians and slaves were thrown into the arena to battle lions or gladiators. Legend tells us that when Telemachus visited the Coliseum and saw gladiators torturing and killing people, he climbed into the arena shouting, "Stop in the name of Jesus. God says do not kill." He was killed on the spot, some say by a gladiator and some say by stoning from the crowd.

5

After this saint's death, Emperor Honorius abolished gladiatorial contests. The last gladiator fight in Rome under Honorius' reign was on January 1st, 404 AD, the date usually cited as the day when St. Telemachus was martyred.

St. Telemachus, you were not afraid to make your voice heard to help erase an evil on the earth, even though you must have known it would mean your death. Why am I sometimes so hesitant to speak up when I see or hear something that goes against my beliefs? I would like to be more like you. Lend me your courage so I can raise my voice against abortion, discrimination, abuse of another human being, or anything else that is against God's commands. St. Telemachus, pray for me.

January 2 St. Basil the Great (329-379) and St. Gregory Nazianzen (329-390)

There are seven canonized saints in St. Basil's family! St. Basil himself, his grandmother, father, mother, two brothers, and a sister. St. Basil's sister, St. Macrina the elder, led him from the practice of law to the religious life. He settled to live as a monk in Pontus and drew many followers to the site of what became the first monastery in Asia Minor. His monastic rules are still used as the basis of monastic life. St. Basil invited his good friend, another canonized saint, St. Gregory, who is famous for his sermons on the Trinity, to join him in his monastery. Both men later left monastic life and fought the doctrine of Arianism, which the Emperor Valens sanctioned. This heresy threatened to divide the church because it denied Christ's divinity. Despite the fact that the two friends were subjected to slander, insults, misunderstanding, and personal suffering, they persevered in turning others away from the heresy and St. Gregory went on to rebuild the faith in Constantinople.

St. Basil and St. Gregory, you refused to obey the emperor disregarding any pain and suffering your refusal cost you. There are many today who belittle Christianity through jokes, cartoons, and disparaging remarks. Do I encourage this kind of irreverence by saying nothing or do I speak out when I witness anyone speaking against or poking fun at my faith, whether friends, family, or strangers? Do I defend the truth as you did? Holy saints, please pray for me that I, like you, have the courage of my convictions.

January 3 St. Genevieve (422-512) played a large part in saving Paris from Attila and the Huns. The people of Paris wanted to run away when they heard Attila was on his way to the city, but St. Genevieve told them, "No, do not run away. Stay

7

and pray for God's protection." When the Parisians followed her urging, their prayers were answered; Attila changed directions and did not attack. This saint spent her life in prayer and practicing charity to others. In fact one of the symbols of St. Genevieve is a loaf of bread signifying her generosity.

Saint Genevieve, you grew close to God through your prayer life and your work with the needy. Your trust in him never failed even when your city was threatened by barbarians. It is hard to give our worries to God and trust that everything will come out according to his plan. How strong is my trust in the Lord? Do I give my concerns to him and spend my time helping others instead of worrying uselessly? Please pray, St. Genevieve, that my prayers and generosity to others cement my trust in God.

January 4 St. Elizabeth Seton (1774-1821) was left with five children to support when her husband died. She was just 30 years old. The next year, 1805, she converted to Catholicism and moved to Baltimore to open a school for Catholic girls. In 1809 she started the Sisters of Charity. This saint's life was full of grief: the early death of her mother and a younger sister, her husband's death at an early age and the death of two daughters, the heartbreak of friends and family turning away from her when

she became Catholic, and the difficulty of a troubled son. She trusted in God and met all adversity in a positive, hopeful way. She was canonized in 1975, the first American saint.

St. Elizabeth, you never lost faith that God would see you through your many sorrows and pain. Instead of complaining, you accepted the path God chose for you and, not only raised your family as a single mother, but also helped others through the school you opened and the congregation of sisters you founded. Am I a complainer or do I meet troubles with a positive attitude and trust that God will help me through any difficulty? St. Elizabeth, can you pray for me so that I can meet adversity as you did with complete faith that God is holding my hand along the way?

January 5 St. John Neumann (1811-1860) was a great organizer. Born in Europe, he was ordained a priest in New York and used his fluency in seven languages to do missionary work with immigrants in Buffalo, NY. When he was 29 he became a member of the Redemptorists and continued his missionary work in other states as well. As Bishop of Philadelphia, he organized Catholic parish schools into a diocesan structure and attracted many teaching orders to the city increasing the number of schools and students. St. John Neumann was also a prolific

writer; before he died at age 49, he authored two catechisms, a Bible history, and a handbook for priests.

St. John Neumann, you used your talents in many ways: you helped the poor, you organized diocesan schools so they were able to offer a Catholic education to many young people, and you left a legacy of written work for future generations. Matthew 25:14-30 tells of God giving "talents" to three men. One man buried his talents instead of using them wisely and that man was banished into the darkness. What talents has God given me? Am I using those talents in a way that pleases him? Am I using them to spread God's word, bringing others to experience his love? Am I using them to help those who are less fortunate than I? St. John Neumann, pray for me. I want to use my talents wisely.

January 6 Blessed Brother Andre Bessette (1845-1937) was one of 12 children from a poor French Canadian family. Orphaned at age 12, he tried to earn a living at a number of jobs, but his lack of education and chronic pain kept him from being successful. He joined the Congregation of the Holy Cross and served in the humble job of doorkeeper at Notre Dame College in Montreal for 40 years as well as devoting his time to caring for the sick. Brother Andre loved St. Joseph and, raising the money bit by bit, he built a chapel to that saint at Mount

Royal. He was so loved that, when he died, crowds of people came to pay their respects.

Blessed Brother Andre, despite the handicaps that plagued you, you persevered in searching for how you could best serve the Lord and touched the lives of many people with your love. Do I accept setbacks as part of God's plan for me or am I a complainer when things don't go my way? What obstacles am I facing now? Do I look at them as another way God helps me grow strong? Do I consider them a challenge instead of a curse? Blessed Brother Andre, pray for me.

January 7 St. Raymond of Penyafort (1175-1275) was a very busy man for the entire one hundred years he spent on this earth. He earned a doctorate in canon and civil law when he was in his thirties, joined the Dominicans when he was 41, and then went to Rome to be confessor to Pope Gregory IX. Part of his work there was to compile all the decrees of popes and councils made in the eighty years since it had last been done. The five books he compiled were considered the best organized collection of church law for almost 500 years. When St. Raymond was 60, he became archbishop of Tarragona and, at age 63, was chosen to lead the Dominicans. He retired at age 65 but not to rest; he spent the remainder of his life opposing

heresy and working for the conversion of the Moors.

St. Raymond, you accomplished so much in your lifetime. I complain sometimes that I don't have the time for everything I have to do, but I know that, if I didn't procrastinate or whittle away my time, I would get everything done with time to spare. How can I make better use of my time today and everyday from now on so that I can fulfill God's expectations and wishes for me to live a full and productive life? St. Raymond, pray for me.

January 8 St. Apollinaris (died c. 175) was a bishop in the second century when the church was being persecuted under Emperor Marcus Aurelius. In order to stop the persecution, St. Apollinaris reminded the emperor of how the Christians had helped him defeat the Germans. When, in the middle of a very dry period, the Roman legions were dying from lack of water, Christians, who formed one of the legions, fell to their knees and prayed for rain. It fell almost immediately enabling the Romans to be victorious.

St. Apollinaris, you did not hesitate to remind the Emperor of how God helped him when in battle. Sometimes I need reminding that everything I have was given me by God. How do I show I am grateful? Do I remember to pray before every meal in thanksgiving for the food He has provided, every morning for the brand new day ahead of me, and every night for bringing me safely through the day? St. Apollinaris, pray for me that I never take God's gifts for granted and that I might be an example to others in giving thanks to God.

January 9 St. Adrian of Canterbury (635-710) was born in Africa and, after refusing the office of Archbishop of Canterbury, he traveled to Italy to become abbot of Saints Peter and Paul Monastery outside of Naples. During his 39 years there, he developed a famous center of learning that attracted scholars from all over the world. St. Adrian died on January 9 and was buried in the monastery. When the monastery was renovated many years later, his body was discovered in an unspoiled state, and his tomb became famous for the miracles that occurred there.

St. Adrian, two of the things that you are remembered for are the center of learning you developed and the miracles that took place at your tomb. Learning about God and our faith and sharing that knowledge can cause miracles to happen, miracles that can bring me and others around me closer to God. How often do I read books about my faith or discuss my beliefs with others? Do I listen and try to learn from sermons at church services or do I let my mind wander? Do I look for answers to questions I have about my faith whether from leaders at my church or from the catechism or bible? St. Adrian, pray for me.

13

January 10 St. William of Bourges (1155-1209) was a Cistercian, a humble man who did not care for the pleasures of the world. Because he knew that becoming the Archbishop of Bourges would put him in the public eye, he refused the office until the Pope and the head of the Cistercians commanded that he accept. After he became archbishop, he intensified his sacrifices and self-mortification because he said that now he had to suffer for all in his charge. When he was ready to die, he asked to be placed on a bed of ashes in a hair shirt. So many miracles took place at his tomb at the Cathedral Church of Bourges, the monks could not record them all.

St. William, you were a very humble and self-sacrificing person. No matter what you did for your people, you never asked for recognition or thanks. It's human to want the good we do here on earth acknowledged, but a heavenly reward is the best recognition. Do I have the strength of will, as you did, to help others just because it's the right thing to do? Do I offer help even if I'm given no credit or gratitude in return? Do I take these words from 1 Corinthians 10:31 to heart: "So, whether you eat or drink or whatever you do, do everything for the glory of God."? St. William, pray for me.

◇< ◇< ◇<

January 11 St. Theodosius the Cenobiarch (c. 529) went on a pilgrimage from his native Turkey to Jerusalem and stayed to enter a monastery. For a long time, he worked to oppose a heresy with such success that the Emperor, who favored the heresy, exiled him. Later in his life, he decided to live the life of a hermit near the Dead Sea, but so many followed him that he established a monastery there made up of several churches for people of different nationalities. Note: The title Cenobiarch means "Leader of a Cenobitical Society," a monastery where the monks did not have to seclude themselves from the world.

St. Theodosius, you wanted to live a quiet life with just a few close followers but, when many others wanted to join you, you gave up your dream and opened your doors to people from all over the world. Sometimes duty calls us to do something, like taking care of an aging parent or a sick relative, which is hard because it means we have to make sacrifices and give up a part of our lives. Please pray for me so that, when someone looks to me for help, I give them my hand as willingly and as graciously as you did.

January 12 St. Marguerite Bourgeoys (1620-1700) accepted an invitation from the governor of Montreal to travel from her native France to Canada to become a teacher in New France. After giving away her inheritance, she sailed to the New World and a new adventure. She opened her first school in 1658 and, as her mission grew, took the perilous journey back

to France four times to recruit more teachers. St. Marguerite organized the group of teachers into the Congregation of Notre Dame, an order of nuns that included the French recruits as well as Canadian and Native American women. The sisters survived the dangers of the wilderness and lack of supplies to start schools for Indian girls in Montreal and Quebec, run missions, open a vocational school, and care for the orphan girls that the French King sent to the New World to become the wives and mothers of pioneers.

Saint Marguerite, you were not frightened by the prospect of a dangerous ocean trip or a life in the New World. You accepted the challenge and willingly gave of yourself to help others. When I am faced with a challenge, especially if accepting it means I can be of service to someone, how do I respond? Do I always put myself first or am I willing to sacrifice some comfort if it will help someone through a hard time? St. Marguerite, please pray for me, that my response to challenges will always be as brave and as big-hearted as yours was.

January 13 Saint Hilary of Poitiers (315-368) was one of the many holy men who spent their lives fighting Arianism, the heresy that denied the divinity of Christ. After he was chosen to be the Bishop of Poitiers, France, the Emperor Constantius demanded that all the bishops of the west condemn Athanasius

who was a powerful enemy of the heresy. St. Hilary refused and was exiled from France for years before being allowed to return. He never wavered in his defense of the church's doctrines even when he was called a "disturber of the peace."

St. Hilary, you fought for what you believed was right and did not compromise your beliefs even when you were forced to leave your country. Compromise can be a valuable tool when settling disputes, but not when applied to our faith. Have I ever compromised my beliefs for any reason? Do I allow myself to get into situations where I might be tempted to compromise them? Do I always and everywhere give voice to what I believe? St. Hilary, please pray that I remain strong in my faith even if doing so brings me grief.

January 14 St. Felix of Nola (died c. 255) was arrested, beaten, and jailed in the year 250, when the Emperor Decius began persecuting Christians with vehemence. One night an angel came to him telling him to go help his bishop, Maximus. His shackles fell off and the cell door unlocked. He rescued his ailing bishop and then fled pursued by soldiers. Spying a hole in the ground he jumped in and a spider spun a web over the opening. The soldiers passed by, thinking the hole was empty because the web was unbroken.

St. Felix of Nola, God intervened in your life these two

17

times to save you from your persecutors. How many times has God intervened in my life to save me from some misfortune, times I don't even know about? I know that God loves me and cares for me every day and that He wants the best for me. How am I showing my gratitude for his care—in prayers of thanksgiving, in giving to others, in spending some time each day quietly adoring him, in living my life to its fullest? St. Felix, pray for me.

January 15 St. Paul the Hermit (239-342) was born into a wealthy family, but his parents died when he was about 16 years old. When he learned that someone in his family was going to report him to the emperor as a Christian, he hid in a cave to avoid persecution. He found that he enjoyed the solitary life and remained there until he died. When St. Antony heard about St. Paul, he visited him and was the person who buried him.

St. Paul, you renounced all worldly things and spent your life in contemplative silence. Do I ever take a few minutes to sit silently so that God can make his presence known to me? When can I find a few minutes of quiet time today clearing my mind of all thoughts and letting God's love flow over me? St. Paul the Hermit, pray for me.

inspiration to me. Am I brave enough to speak about Jesus and his love for us to nonbelievers? If not, what is holding me back? Do my actions bring others to God or turn them away from him? What can I do today to show Jesus that I want to follow his command to spread his word? St. Sebastian, pray for me.

January 21 St. Agnes (d. 304) was only 12 years old when she was martyred. Legend says that she was given up to the Romans as a Christian because she refused the attentions of a young Roman. When Roman officials told her that she had to offer worship to their false gods, she told them, "I will not do that." Instead, she prayed out loud to the one true God as Roman soldiers whipped her and dragged her through the streets.

St Agnes, you were so young and yet you stayed true to your beliefs. You refused to give witness to false gods. Am I worshipping any false gods? Do I put wealth, fame, popularity, or power before God? Have I ever acted against my beliefs in order to achieve those things? Do I live my life in a way that shows I believe that only God lasts forever and it is only He whom we must worship and serve? St. Agnes, pray for me. I want to put God before all things of this earth.

January 22 St. Vincent of Saragossa (died 304) served as deacon to Bishop Valerius of Saragossa. The two men were brought to trial for their beliefs but, since the Bishop had a speech defect, St. Vincent spoke for them both. His self-assured manner of speaking enraged the governor and he was imprisoned and tortured for his faith while the Bishop was exiled. Even while St. Vincent suffered in prison, he managed to convert one of his jailers by acting as all Christians should, with love and kindness. He was offered release from prison if he would allow books of scripture to be thrown into the fire. He refused and was martyred.

St. Vincent of Saragossa, while you were suffering torture in prison, you put your pain aside and led another person to God. Am I dwelling on what's wrong with my life instead of what's right with it? Is the cup always half-full or half-empty to me? Do I give my problems to God, confident that He will take care of them, instead of wasting time worrying? Do I repay him for his care and gifts by being a good example to others? St. Vincent, pray for me as I follow God's plan for me with complete trust.

January 23 St. Ildephonsus (c. 607- 667) was a prolific writer best known for devotion to and his writing

about the Blessed Virgin Mary and his history of the Spanish Church. He believed that no one could serve Jesus without serving Mary. This saint was a favorite subject for medieval artists because of a legend that the Blessed Mother appeared to him and gave him a chalice. Despite the opposition of his family, St. Ildephonsus became a monk and served as abbot of his monastery. He was later elected Archbishop of Toledo, Spain, acting faithfully in that capacity until his death.

St. Ildephonsus, you were very devoted to the Blessed Virgin Mary and remained steadfast to that devotion all your life. Do I understand how much our heavenly mother loves me? Do I go to her when I am troubled so that she might intercede with her son for me? Mary has asked so little of us, only to recite the rosary for peace. Can I make time each day to pray to her as you did? St. Ildephonsus, pray for me.

January 24 Saint Francis de Sales (1567-1622) became seriously depressed when he was 18 years old fearing that he had lost God's grace and was doomed to hate him with the damned for all eternity. While praying before the statue of Our Lady to whom he had previously dedicated himself, his fear

and despair left him. He went on to earn his doctorate in law and then entered the priesthood becoming a productive writer. His pamphlets explaining Church doctrine encouraged many conversions.

Saint Francis, how dark your days must have been when you felt you had lost your love for God. You turned to Our Lady and she didn't fail you. Despair and loss of faith are tricks the devil plays on us, hoping he will win us to his side. Do I ever let doubts about God and his loving care cloud my spirit or, when I can't see my way to God, do I turn to Jesus and his mother for help saying, "Jesus, mercy," or "Mary, my mother, help me believe." ? St. Francis, pray for me.

January 25 The Conversion of St. Paul (1ˢᵗ century)

St. Paul was a relentless persecutor of Christians until the day he and some companions, on the road to Damascus, were surrounded by a light. As they fell to the ground, Paul, or Saul as he was known then, heard Jesus asking him why he was persecuting his people. Jesus told him to go to Damascus where he stayed for three days, blinded, and without food or drink. God then sent Ananias, a Christian, to cure Paul's blindness, baptize him, and tell him that God wanted him to bear witness to him. St. Paul took up his task wholeheartedly. Before he died he said, "I have fought a good fight; I have finished my course; I have kept the faith."

St. Paul, when God opened your eyes to his love, you embraced the faith and helped many others come to know, love, and serve God. Your life shows us that it is never too late for anyone to become a servant of God. How am I fighting the good fight? How am I spreading God's word? Do my words and actions show others how much God loves me and how much I love him in return? Will I someday be able to say, as you did, "I have kept the faith"?

January 26 Sts. Timothy (died c. 97) and Titus (died c.94) were good friends of St. Paul. Timothy was a convert who worked with St. Paul for fifteen years often taking on difficult situations in the churches that St. Paul founded. He was born of a Greek father and a Jewish mother and therefore the Jews considered him "illegitimate." His report to St. Paul on the Church at Thessalonica led to the letter that St. Paul wrote to the Thessalonians. Titus, a Greek gentile, was a peacemaker who carried a harsh letter from St. Paul to the troublesome community at Corinth, and he was the one who calmed the situation there. He was sent to Crete to organize the Church and later served as the first Bishop of Crete.

Saints Timothy and Titus, neither of you hesitated to carry out hard tasks given you by St. Paul for the good of the Church. You realized that nothing is too hard if you have faith that God is with you. When I am facing something that I fear is going to be difficult, do I follow your example and go ahead with courage? Do I trust that God will not let me down? Can I imitate you and put myself and all my fears into his loving arms? Sts. Timothy and Titus, pray for me.

January 27 St. Angela Merici (1474-1540) became aware that many youngsters were not being taught about the faith, so she converted her home into a school and began teaching young girls about Christianity. Eventually she gathered other like-minded women around her and, taking St. Ursula as their patroness, founded the Ursuline Sisters, a teaching order of nuns who were the first nuns to work outside the cloister. Once, on a pilgrimage, she lost her eyesight but continued on her trip without complaint. On the return voyage, in the exact spot where she had been blinded, God restored her sight.

St. Angela, you recognized a problem of your time and you did everything you could to solve it. You have only to listen to the news to realize there are many problems in our world today. Are there any problems affecting people I know or society as a whole that I, in some small way, can address? How can I make my life an example of compassionate giving of myself and encourage others to do the same? St. Angela Merici, pray for me.

January 28 St Thomas Aquinas (1225-1274) wanted to become part of the Order of Preachers, the Dominicans, even though his family wanted him to become an abbot with the Benedictine monks. His family kidnapped him and locked him up for over a year. The Pope commanded the family not to stand in his way, and he was allowed to resume his vocation. St. Thomas was a brilliant man as well as a prolific writer of treatises, poems, books, and music like the well-known *Tantum Ergo* and *O Salutaris*. His *Summa Theologiae*, although never finished, stands as the most thorough explanation of theological teaching. His nickname, Doctor Angelicus, means "the teacher who is like an angel."

St. Thomas Aquinas, you were brilliant and talented, and you used all your genius and gifts to serve God and to explain God's truths to others. I believe that God gives each one of us whatever we need to serve him and spread his word. What talents has God given me that I can use for his glory? Is there a

ministry at church or in my community where I can volunteer
my help and do some good in his name? Will I choose to use my
talent to serve him? If not, why not? St. Thomas, pray for me.

January 29 Servant of God Brother Juniper (died c.
1258) had a very generous and compassionate heart. Not much is
known of this man's early life, but we do know that he joined the
Franciscan Friars in 1210 and his fellow friars learned not to
leave anything around because Brother Juniper would give it
away. After he had been forbidden to give away any more of his
clothing, Brother Juniper met a poor man who needed a cloak.
Being both obedient and compassionate at the same time, he told
the beggar, "I have been forbidden to give you my cloak, but, if
you take it from me, I will not stop you."

Brother Juniper, you were a simple man devoted to Jesus
and helping others. When you saw people in need, you helped
them. That sounds so easy but, in reality, unselfish giving involves
sacrifice whether of goods or time. Is there someone I know who
has a need right now that I could meet even if it means making a
sacrifice? Am I using my time, talent, and worldly goods to help
others? How can I follow your example of caring for God's
children with loving care? Brother Juniper, pray for me.

prophecy as God's will. Sometimes I think that some rules are not made for me because I'm too good, or too smart, or too…… whatever, but that's when I need to look to your example. God's commandments are for all, not just for some. Period! Can I follow his commands without complaint knowing that, by doing so, I ensure a place with him in Heaven?

February 3 St. Blaise (martyred C. 316 AD) is remembered on this day by the rite of the Blessing of the Throats that takes place in Catholic churches. Two blessed candles are crossed and held against the throat as the priest says a blessing. Legend has it that St. Blaise, a member of a group of men called the holy helpers because they used their healing powers to help others, saved the life of a boy who had swallowed a fish bone. Because of this, he became the patron saint of those who suffer from illnesses of the throat.

St. Blaise, you were a healer. Although I do not have your healing powers, there are many ways I can help those who are sick. Realizing that emotional healing goes hand-in-hand with physical healing, do I help ailing friends by showing them I care? Do I make the time to treat with patience and love those around me who are suffering? Am I quick to offer a kind word, a smile, or an offer of help when I see someone hurting? St. Blaise, pray for me. I want to be a compassionate helper.

February 4 St. Joan of Valois, (1464-1505) was the daughter of King Louis XI of France. Her father did not like her, perhaps because her body was deformed, and sent her away when she was five. Although St. Joan wished to enter the religious life, she was married to the Duke of Orleans when she was twelve. The Duke was cruel to her and, when he became King Louis XII, he asked that the marriage be annulled. It was, on the grounds that there had been no mutual consent to the union. St. Joan gladly accepted the annulment and went on to found the Sisters of the Annunciation.

St. Joan, despite the fact that two important men in your life treated you badly, you held on to your dream of becoming a religious and lived to see your dreams come true. You are the perfect example that what you make of your life depends on you, not anyone else. Do I take full responsibility for my life or do I blame others if I am unhappy? Hard work and prayer make any dream possible. Do I give my all in effort and in prayer for a fulfilled life? St. Joan, pray for me.

February 5 St. Agatha (died c. 251) is said to have been a young, beautiful, and rich young woman dedicated to God at the time that an emperor issued edicts against the Christians. When charges were brought against her for being a Christian, a magistrate told her he would exchange sex for dropping charges against her. She refused and was sent to a brothel where she again refused to "entertain" anyone even though she was tortured, beaten, had her breasts crushed and cut off, and was rolled over hot coals.

What suffering you endured, St. Agatha! Such strength had to come from your faith in and love for God. Any suffering I may have ever had seems so trivial compared to yours. Do I ever think of offering my pain, whether emotional or physical, up to God instead of feeling self-pity? Is there any pain that I am feeling today that I can offer up in thanksgiving for his everlasting love? Do I ever thank God for the opportunity to suffer for him? St. Agatha, pray for me.

February 6 St. Paul Miki and Companions (d. 1597) were crucified because they preached about God's love for mankind. St. Paul Miki was a Jesuit and his companions were 25 Japanese Christians. Even while he was dying on the cross, St. Paul Miki continued to preach telling of the love Jesus has

37

for us all and thanking God for being able to witness to him. He forgave his persecutors and asked all who were present at his death to continue to love and serve God.

St. Paul Miki, you were able to continue your work for God even when you were dying on the cross, and you followed Christ's lead when you forgave your enemies. Do I ever follow your example and make a conscious effort to teach others about God's love? Do I model his love through my words and actions? Do I forgive those who may have hurt me in some way? Do I pray for those I don't particularly admire or like? St. Paul Miki, pray for me.

February 7 St. Richard of Lucca (died c. 722), an under-king of the west Saxons, is best known as the father of three saints: sons, Willibald, evangelist and author, and Winnebald, abbot, and a daughter, Walburga, who was an abbess and author. St. Richard was on a pilgrimage to Rome with his two sons when he became ill and died at Lucca. He was buried there and many miracles were reported at his tomb. The people of Lucca held him in great esteem calling him "King of the English."

St. Richard, you raised three children who went on to live holy lives that merited them sainthood. Just as it is today, it was hard in your day to raise children to know, love, and serve God and to make him the center of their lives. How am I teaching the children in my life about God's love for us and his wish that we love him in return? Can I listen more and talk less? Can I pay attention to what is going on in their lives and get to know their friends? Can I ask God's help in this most important job of my life? St. Richard, help me imitate your example of parenthood. Pray for me.

February 8 St. Josephine Bakhita (1869-1947) was kidnapped from her home in Olgossa, a village in Darfur, Sudan, Africa, and sold into slavery when she was six years old. After many years of cruelty and suffering, she was sold to the Italian Consul Callisto Legnani who treated her kindly. St. Josephine accompanied the consul when he returned to Italy, and she found work there as a nanny for another family. Through this family she came to stay with the Canossian Daughters of Charity in Venice. In 1890 she was baptized, confirmed, and received Holy Communion. In 1896 she became a Canossian Sister.

St. Josephine, you were deprived of your freedom for many years, but instead of becoming bitter, you became strong as you turned to God. My troubles are nothing compared to yours, yet sometimes I do not see that they strengthen me and bring me closer to God. Do I really trust that God will never give me more than I can bear and that He shares my burdens? Do I look at my trials and troubles as pathways to Heaven? Do I offer them to God in thanksgiving? St. Josephine, pray for me and for the terrible trials the people in your native Darfur endure even today.

February 9 Blessed Marianus Scotus (d. 1088) started off from Ireland for a pilgrimage, never thinking he would end up staying in Germany to become a Benedictine monk. While he was passing through that country on the way to Rome, this accomplished calligrapher was asked to copy some manuscripts. He agreed and, when his task was completed, he stayed to join the Benedictines and founded St. Peter's abbey, becoming its first abbot. He returned to Ireland and persuaded so many other devout young Irishmen to join him that 12 other monasteries developed.

Opportunities to do God's work can spring up anywhere! Blessed Marianus Scotus, you were wise enough to recognize God's call and answer, "Yes, I will." What opportunities is God presenting to me now to make his world a better place? Am I ignoring the chance to do good because I'm too busy or too protective of my own comfort? How would my life change if I looked for opportunities to do something for God? Blessed Marianus Scotus, pray for me.

February 10 St. Scholastica (480-542) was the twin sister of St. Benedict. Like Benedict, she too started a religious community situating it not far from her brother's monastery. Brother and sister were close but only visited each other once each year spending their time together discussing spiritual matters. When St. Scholastica died, St. Benedict, although he was at his monastery, saw her spirit rising from her body and announced her death to his brothers.

St. Scholastica, you and your twin were close in spirit and I'm sure you would have liked to see him more often. Yet you gave up the earthly pleasure of his visits to become closer to God. Sacrifice is never easy, but whatever pain we feel from our sacrifices here on earth is nothing compared to the glory we will have when we are finally with God. How can I make some sacrifice each day that will bring me closer to Jesus? Can I make time to call a sick friend, give up a dessert, offer someone a ride, or make some other sacrifice? Can I follow your unselfish example? St. Scholastica, pray for me.

February 11 *Our Lady of Lourdes (1858-appearance)*
appeared, on this day, to a young girl at a spot close to Lourdes, France. On February 11, 1858, Bernadette Soubirous saw a lady dressed in a white robe and a blue girdle holding a rosary who identified herself as "the Immaculate Conception." At the Lady's request, Bernadette dug and found a well whose water has proved to have powers to cure body and spirit although scientists can't explain why. The shrine built at Lourdes where Our Lady appeared has become a place where pilgrims flock and where many healings have taken place.

Our Blessed Mother, through your intercession, many people have been cured of their illnesses. You are good to your children and we thank you for your love. Even if I can't visit your shrine at Lourdes, I know that you intercede for me when I tell you about my needs just as I know my prayers will be answered in God's own way. I trust you and your Son to know what is best for me and for my spiritual life. I love you, Blessed Mother. Please pray for me.

February 12 *St. Apollonia (died c. 249)* was a Christian at a time when heathens turned against believers, torturing them in many bloody and painful ways. St. Apollonia was asked to repeat words which were contrary to her beliefs as a Christian

and she refused. First all her teeth were broken and then she was taken to a blazing fire and threatened with a fiery death. She managed to become free of her captors and ran into the fire voluntarily.

St. Apollonia, you chose to give up your life rather than say even one word against God. I think that every time his name is used as a curse must hurt him so much and yet what do I choose to do when I hear people using God's name in vain? Do I ignore it, or do I get my courage up and tell them that their use of his name in any context other than a prayer is disrespectful? I respect the beliefs of others; do I expect and ask them to respect mine? St. Apollonia, pray for me.

February 13 St. Catherine de Ricci (1522-1590) lived during the time of the Reformation when there were many corrupt people in high positions in the Church. It would have been easy for St. Catherine to go along with the general corruption, but she opted to join an order of nuns who wanted to reform the church. This saint, so humble and holy despite the secular times she lived in, was given the honor of the stigmata and also experienced each week the passion of Christ. She was also known to be able to be in two places at one time.

St. Catherine, you ignored the decadence around you

and concentrated on God. If all Christians had followed your example, the Church would not have been torn apart as it was during the Reformation. Setting a good example is important in any day and age. Do my words and actions reflect my love of God as yours did? Is what I do and say turning others toward or away from God? St. Catherine de Ricci, pray for me. I want to be a good model of God's love.

February 14 Sts. Cyril and Methodius (died 869; died 884) were two brothers from Greece who became teachers and missionaries to the Slavs. Methodius was a governor of Greece and Cyril was asked to be a governor but refused. Both entered the monastery and taught the Slavs about Christianity, translating Holy Scripture using a Slavic alphabet St. Cyril designed. Methodius also translated the Bible. The Cyrillic alphabet that replaced St. Cyril's alphabet was named for him by one of his disciples who invented it.

Sts. Cyril and Methodius, you went out into the world to spread the word of God. As St. Paul says, "How beautiful are the feet of those who preach the gospel of peace; of those who bring glad tidings of good things." You are blessed for your work. Am I following your example and spreading God's word? Do I tell others of my joy in God, of my certainty that

He is preparing an unimaginably beautiful place for me after I leave this life? Do I share the story of Jesus' sacrificial love? Do I always remember that I am God's voice here on earth? Sts. Cyril and Methodius, pray for me.

February 15 St. Claude de la Colombiere (1641-1682) was a Jesuit priest who preached devotion to the Sacred Heart of Jesus. Sent to England to be preacher for the Duchess of York, he brought many fallen away Catholics back to the church through his words and actions. His health began failing and, when he was suspected of plotting against the king and thrown into prison, the conditions in the prison made his condition worse. Banished from England, he returned to France to die.

St. Claude, you brought so many fallen away Catholics back to the church. There are many Catholics today who have strayed from the church, some even in my family. Do I try to understand what is going on in their hearts? Do I offer up prayers for their return to Christ's church? Do I talk to them about the faith and invite them to church functions? Do I offer them books that give information and inspiration? St. Claude, pray that my words and actions help bring the stray sheep back into the fold.

February 16 St. Onesimus (died c. 95) was a slave who offended his master and fled to St. Paul who was then imprisoned. Paul baptized him and then asked his master to free him and allow him to become one of Paul's assistants. St. Onesimus served St. Paul, in one instance by helping to deliver the Epistle to the Colossians, and went on to become an ardent preacher of the gospel and Bishop of Ephesus. He was tortured for 18 days by the governor of Rome and then stoned to death because of his preaching.

St. Onesimus, when you were frightened, you fled to St. Paul, and he helped you. We too have a friend to turn to when we are troubled and life's burdens seem too heavy. God is always there for us. He loves us as his children and wants the best for us. He will never let us down. Do I turn to God when I am troubled instead of fretting and worrying and feeling alone? How can I remind myself that God is happy to help me carry my burdens? What burden shall I ask him to carry for me today? St. Onesimus, pray for me.

February 17 Founders of the Orders of Servites (1233)
Around 1233, on the Feast of the Assumption, Our Blessed Virgin Mary appeared to seven young men in Florence and told them she wanted them to leave their homes, adopt the

Rule of St. Augustine, and found the order of her servants. The men did as she asked, and the Order of the Servites spread rapidly over Europe. The main goals of the order were to sanctify its members, preach the Gospel, and encourage devotion to Mary. In 1249, the order was officially approved by the Church.

You were seven men who left everything you owned behind and joined together to obey Our Blessed Mother's wishes. I know that Mary loves me as a mother loves her child and, if I follow her example of what a servant of God should be, I will come to no harm in this world or the next. Do I listen, as you did, and do what Our Lady wants me to do? Do I pray the rosary as she has asked? Do I show her the respect she deserves as both my mother and the mother of God? Saintly seven, pray for me.

February 18 Blessed John of Fiesole (1400-1455) is better known to the world as Fra Angelica, artist and Dominican friar. He began his study of art as a young boy and become famous for his use of vibrant color and his lifelike figures that inspired religious devotion. His most famous works are the "Descent from the Cross" and the "Annunciation." Fra Angelica joined the Dominicans when he was 20 years old and

held many leadership positions within the order although he refused to become Archbishop of Florence because he preferred to remain out of the limelight.

Fra Angelica, you used the talent that God gave you to inspire all who saw your work to feel closer to God and to heaven. God gives everyone talents although it may take time to discover what those talents are. What talent has God given me? How can I use it to further his glory and make the world a better place? Fra Angelica, help me to recognize the talent God has given me and show me how I can best use it to serve him and my fellow man. Please pray for me.

February 19 St. Conrad of Piacenza (d. 1351), born into a noble family, was hunting one day when he ordered his attendants to set fire to some brush to flush out game hiding there. Winds caused the fire to blaze up and spread, destroying the surrounding land. A beggar was accused of the crime, arrested, and sentenced to death. When the poor man was being led to his execution, St. Conrad confessed that he was the guilty one. He had to sell all that he owned in order to make up for the damage he had done and was left a pauper. He became a hermit and his wife joined the poor Clares. Many miracles were attributed to him during his lifetime.

St. Conrad, you could not let an innocent man be punished for what you did so, although your punishment was very harsh, you confessed your guilt. You did the right thing. Do I ever not do the right thing because of laziness, fear of what others may think, or lack of compassion? I want always to do what is right, but I am weak. Please pray for me, St. Conrad, that I might follow your example and do the right thing no matter how hard it is.

February 20 Blessed Jacinta (1910-1920) and Francisco Marto (1908-1919) and their cousin, Lucia Santo, spent their days in the fields near the little town of Fatima in Portugal watching the families' sheep. On May 13 of 1917, a year when Europe was in the midst of a great war, Our Blessed Mother appeared to the three and asked them to return to the spot where she appeared on the 13th of each month for six months. She also asked them to say the rosary for peace and for the conversion of Russia where the czar, Nicholas II, had just been overthrown. Just a few years after the final apparition in October of 1917, Jacinta and Francisco died of influenza and were beatified in 2000. Lucia, who became a nun, died in 2005 at the age of 97. Millions of people today visit the shrine of Our Lady of Fatima.

49

Blessed Jacinta, Blessed Francisco, and Lucia, you were privileged to see Our Blessed Mother while you were still here on earth, and you carried her message to the world. Our world is still troubled today and, more than ever, we need to pray and work for peace. Am I working to promote peace within my family and friends and at my work place? Please join your prayers with mine for understanding between peoples and nations so fighting and war will become a thing of the past.

February 21 St Peter Damian (1007-1072) had a very difficult childhood—his mother refused to nurse him, he was orphaned, and the brother who raised him was cruel. St Peter Damien was finally rescued by a kinder brother and sent to school. He became a professor but left teaching to become a Benedictine monk and later founded a hermitage. Believing that the clergy had become too worldly, he encouraged them to lead a more disciplined life and he fought against simony, the practice of selling spiritual benefits. He was a prolific writer and successful mediator and is a Doctor of the Church.

St. Peter Damian, so often people blame their parents or poor beginnings for all the failures in their lives. Trusting in God, you moved on with your life, forgave those that caused you unhappiness or pain, and concentrated on the future, not the past. Do I forgive anyone who has caused me pain? Do I let go of past hurts or do I brood on them? Is there something in my life right now that I need to give over to God so I can learn to forgive and forget? Do I believe that forgiveness will lead me to peace within myself? St. Peter Damian, pray for me.

February 22 Feast of the Chair of St. Peter the Apostle refers to the occupant of the chair, not the chair itself. We celebrate Jesus choosing St. Peter to be the rock-like foundation upon which He would build his church on earth despite the fact that St. Peter had denied Jesus three times before the crucifixion. Jesus looked beyond St. Peter's faults and saw a man who could be a spokesperson not only for the twelve apostles but for the whole church. St. Peter was crucified around 64 AD head down because he said he was not worthy to hang on the cross as Jesus did.

Sweet Jesus, you chose St. Peter, a very human man, to lead your church on earth. Like Peter, I too have faults and temptations that I fight, sometimes unsuccessfully. Look beyond my faults, dear Jesus, and know that I love you with my whole heart. Help me see how I can keep your word and share it with others.

February 23 St. Polycarp (d. 156) was a disciple of Saint John the Evangelist and from him heard many stories of when Jesus walked the earth. As Bishop of Smyrna in the second century he faced many problems for, after all the first generation Christians had died, many heresies sprang up as well as controversies about church liturgy. In addition, St. Polycarp served as bishop under a government that hated and persecuted Christians. The saint decided that the best way to address all controversies was to imitate Christ; he was stern with heretics but kind and understanding when Christians disagreed on church matters. When St. Polycarp was 86 years old, he was taken to an arena in Smyrna to be burned at the stake, but the flames would not devour him. Instead he was killed with a dagger and then his body was burned.

St. Polycarp, your decision to imitate Jesus helped you through the many difficulties you experienced in leading your flock to Christ. What difficult situation am I facing now? Have I turned to Jesus for help and asked him what He would do in my situation? Do I believe I can overcome any difficulty as long as I trust in him? WWJD is not just a slogan; it's a way to think through problems and resolve them in a Christian way. St. Polycarp, pray for me.

February 24 St. Ethelbert (d. 616) became King of Kent when he was a teenager. He married a Christian princess named Bertha who came from Paris and brought along with her a chaplain. St. Ethelbert allowed her to practice her religion and, after he had met St. Augustine who had come to England to spread God's word, he became a Christian too. While he encouraged his subjects to practice the faith, he did not force anyone to do so. He became the caretaker of the Church in England, credited with being responsible for the success of Augustine's mission in England.

St. Ethelbert, you were a tolerant man. You neither made your wife give up her faith nor, when you became a Christian yourself, forced any of your subjects to accept your newfound faith. I see intolerance around me today between races, religions, and societal classes. Do I pretend I do not see instances of intolerance or do I have the courage to speak against it? Is my life an example of tolerant behavior as yours was? St. Ethelbert, pray for me.

February 25 St. Tarasius (d. 806) served as Secretary of State to King Constantine, ignoring the excesses of the court and living a very spiritual and spartan life. He was chosen to become Patriarch of Constantinople at a time when the church

at Constantinople was at odds with the Roman church over the veneration of images. He said he would only accept the position if the two churches would come together in a ecumenical council. The veneration of images became an accepted practice as St. Tarasius had hoped and unity was restored for a time.

St. Tarasius, you denied yourself all the worldly pleasures that could have been yours at court and devoted your life to spiritual causes like taking care of the poor and bringing unity to the church. I take for granted the many blessings I have such as a roof over my head and enough food so that I do not go hungry. Is there some pleasure I could give up, even if only for a day, so I can offer up the sacrifice to God for peace between nations and for all those in the world who are not as blessed as I? St. Tarasius, pray for me.

February 26 St. Porphyry of Gaza (353-421) spent five years in the famous desert monastery of Skete in Egypt and five years in a cave on the Jordan River in Palestine before he became very ill and decided to spend his last days in Jerusalem visiting the sites of Christ's passion. While there, he was cured of his illness. Giving away all his belongings, he learned to make shoes and earned his living as a cobbler until he was made a bishop of Gaza without his consent and, in fact, against

his wishes. After consecration, however, he led his flock to the best of his ability and is credited with converting many pagans and ridding the area of pagan statues and temples. He is also remembered for his generosity to the poor.

St. Porphyry, you were given a job you did not want, yet you accepted it and did your best for the Christians under your wing. We all have tasks in life that fall to us by default, responsibilities we would never have chosen for ourselves. Perhaps we must tend to a sick relative, help a friend who is facing hard times, or counsel a rebellious child. When I am faced with a job I do not want, do I react as you did, doing my duty in the best way possible with a generous spirit? Do I carry out my responsibilities cheerfully, without complaint? St. Porphyry, pray for me.

February 27 St. Gabriel of Our Lady of Sorrows (1838-1862) was cured of two serious illnesses before he decided that God was calling him to serve him. Having been educated by the Jesuits, he applied to join that order when he was only 17 years old but, perhaps because of his young age, was refused admittance. He ultimately joined the Passionist Order and, during his novitiate, impressed his superiors by his great attention to obeying God's commands and the Passionate Rule

to the smallest detail as well as his consideration for the feelings of others and his love for the poor. He was devoted to Our Blessed Mother, dwelling particularly on her sorrow at the crucifixion of her son. After this saint's death at age 24 from tuberculosis, many miracles were credited to his intercession and he was canonized in 1920.

St. Gabriel, you were careful to follow the Word of God to the smallest detail. What would my life be like if I did that, if I lived my life exactly as God wants me to? Would solutions to problems and decisions I have to make each day be made easier for me if I asked God first what He would like me to do? Would I get direction from reading his Word? St. Gabriel of Our Lady of Sorrows, pray for me, my family, and my friends so that we might grow closer to God and Mary our mother and live our lives as God would want.

February 28 Blessed Daniel Brottier (1876-1936) was an untiring servant of God. He was ordained a priest and began to teach but, longing to spread the gospel, he became a missionary in Senegal, West Africa. When his health failed, he returned to his native France and helped raise money to build a cathedral in Senegal. His next mission was as a chaplain during World War I where he served with bravery and compassion.

His final work, for 13 years before his death, was caring for orphaned children in a Paris suburb.

Blessed Daniel, it doesn't seem as if you ever took a "time-out" to rest. You led a full life, going from one endeavor to another, and all your good work was done in the name of God. What am I doing with my life to bring glory to his name? Do I dedicate whatever work I do to God? Do I work without complaint and offer it to him? Do I make this world a better place through my good will and love for others? Blessed Daniel, pray for me.

+ March Opening Prayer +

As I continue to learn more about you, Holy Saints, I feel that I learn more about myself as well. I can only pray that this knowledge enriches my service to God and my love for him so that I can more closely imitate your ways. *"Teach us to number our days so that we may arrive at a wisdom of heart." Psalm 89:12*

March 1 St. David of Wales (c. 500-589), the patron saint of Wales, was a teacher and preacher who founded several monasteries in Wales, Cornwall, and Brittany. His monastic rule was very severe. Monks had to plow the fields without the help of animals, drank only water, ate only bread with salt and herbs, owned no possessions, and, in general, lived a very simple life. St. David lived this life himself serving as an example to those who followed him.

St. David, you believed that giving up earthly pleasures brought you closer to God and you inspired others to follow in your footsteps. I know that I would be healthier in both body and spirit if I followed your example and gave up eating and drinking more than I need. What particular food or drink can I give up this week as a sign of my love for God and of respect for my body? St. David, pray for me as I look for a sacrifice I can offer God.

March 2 Blessed Charles the Good (died 1127) was raised from age five by his maternal grandfather after his father, the King of Denmark, was murdered. He inherited his grandfather's title, Count of Flanders, and, in that role, forbade anyone to use the name of God in vain. Blessed Charles was a very just man, making sure that sufficient crops were planted so the poor could have enough food. When he discovered a plot to sell grain to the poor at highly inflated prices, he took steps to put an end to it infuriating the men who had planned on huge profits. Leaders of the plot found him at Mass and beheaded him.

Blessed Charles, you were called the Good because your subjects saw the goodness in you. You cared for your people in all ways, leading them to be mindful of how they used God's name and making sure they had enough to eat. Am

I careful of how I use Our Lord's name? What exactly can I say to let others know how I feel when I hear his name used carelessly? Can I simply say that it saddens me or makes me feel uncomfortable? Will I dare to speak up the next time this happens or will I let fear of what others think of me silence my voice? Blessed Charles, pray for me.

March 3 St. Katharine Drexel (1858-1955), born to a prominent family of Philadelphia, learned from her wealthy and influential parents that she had a responsibility to help those who were needy. Interested in helping black and Native Americans, she not only donated her fortune of about twenty million dollars to further her work but also founded the Sisters of the Blessed Sacrament for Indians and Colored People. She opened the first mission school for Indians in Santa Fe, New Mexico, worked with the Sioux Indians in North and South Dakota, and opened schools for poor African American children in the south. She founded Xavier University in New Orleans, one of the first universities for African Americans in the United States.

St. Katharine Drexel, you sought out and helped those in need, whether the needs were corporal or educational. You made a difference in the lives of many people. I wonder if I have made a difference, if my life has touched anyone as yours did. Is there anything I am doing right now that is making the world a better place? Am I helping the poor, talking to people about God, sharing my time and talent with my church and community?? How can I show God that I love his people, especially those who have not been given the gifts I have? St. Katharine, pray for me.

March 4 St. Casimir (1458-1484) was a prince of Poland raised to serve his father the king, but he chose at an early age to serve God first. Because of his loyalty to God, he ignored the riches of the royal court and lived the simplest of lives wearing plain clothes and sleeping on the floor. He did not want worldly luxuries to lead him away from God. When his father told St. Casimir to lead the army and take over the throne of Hungary, the saint obeyed out of respect for his father, but his heart was not in the battle as he felt it was not the right thing to do. As his soldiers began deserting, St. Casimir returned home, a move that infuriated the king resulting in Casimir's banishment. St. Casimir died from lung disease when he was just 23 years old.

St. Casimir, you could have led a life of luxury, but you gave up worldly pleasures for fear they might take your attention away from God. It is so easy to be taken up with fashionable clothing, bigger houses, newer cars, parties, and trips. There is nothing wrong with wanting to look your best, making a home into a comfortable place to live, providing safe transportation, and enjoying friends and travel, but do I put these things before God? God is the only treasure that is everlasting; all others can be here today but gone by tomorrow. How do I show that I value God above all else? St. Casimir, pray for me.

March 5 St. John Joseph of the Cross (1654-1739) was a modest, humble person. Although of a noble family, he dressed simply and spent much of his time in prayer and fasting. Whenever there was work to be done, this saint always chose the lowliest of tasks and never spared himself when it came to serving others. In fact, when asked to start a friary, he insisted on helping to build it with his own hands. Born on the Feast of the Assumption, he held a life-long devotion to the Blessed Virgin and urged others to become close to her too.

St. John Joseph of the Cross, you were willing to do the meanest of work and never claimed credit for what you did. Your love for the Blessed Mother guided you in your self-sacrificing path. Do I always try to do the work that is easier or more likely to be noticed by others or am I willing to do less desirable jobs? Do I look for credit for everything I do or do I recognize that my successes are made possible by God? Can I follow your example and willingly do any work that has to be done knowing that God's is the only reward that I need. St. John Joseph, pray for me.

March 6 St. Colette (1381-1447) gave her inheritance to the poor when she was orphaned at age 17. Drawn to the religious life, she became an anchoress when she was 21, walled into a cell where the only opening was a small window to a church. While there she had visions that she was to reform the Poor Clares, so she left her cell and began the work she felt called to do. After facing much opposition to the reforms, her work found success. She had the gift of miracles and was greatly devoted to the passion of Christ.

St. Colette, you left your chosen secluded life to take up work that was very difficult. Your love for Christ and his passion helped you as you tried to effect change. It is good to remember that Jesus stands beside us no matter how difficult life can become. We have only to trust in him and his love for us. Is there any worry or hardship, big or small, that I am holding close to me now instead of sharing it with Jesus? Can I

find the trust to ask for his help and believe He is there for me?
St. Colette, pray for me.

March 7 Sts. Perpetua and Felicity (died c. 203) chose
to be imprisoned and sentenced to death rather than renounce
their faith. St. Perpetua was born to a Christian mother and a
pagan father and Felicity was a slave. Both were new mothers:
St. Perpetua had recently had a baby and Felicity gave birth
when in prison. St. Perpetua wrote a diary revealing the
suffering she, Felicity, and several others endured until they
were martyred, the men killed by wild animals, and the women
by having their throats cut. Perpetua's last words to her brother
were, "Stand fast in the faith and love one another."

St. Perpetua and St. Felicity, you and your friends
showed great courage in refusing to worship false gods. Not
only did you face the pain of a brutal death, you also had to
leave your newborn children. Where did such courage come
from? Was it the words of Jesus, "Fear not, I am with you."?
What worries and fears can I put into God's hands right now
with trust that He will give me the courage I need to deal with
them? Saints Perpetua and Felicity, pray for me.

March 8 St. John of God (1495-1550) was a very impulsive person. He ran away from home when he was eight years old and had an adventurous life which included serving in the army, being imprisoned, working as a shepherd and as a servant to a family exiled to Africa, peddling books, and owning a book store. Once he rushed into a burning hospital without thought, saving patients and hospital property. At one point, St. John of God was put away in an insane asylum for his excesses in worship. As soon as he began to recover, he helped the workers at the hospital, and then left to start his own hospital so that inmates would get better treatment than was the standard of the day.

St. John of God, you often chose to follow your impulses as when you began caring for the sick in the streets of Granada and founded a hospital even though you were penniless. How often have I had an impulse to help someone in need and then talked myself out of it because of doubts of my ability or worry of how I might look to others? How often have I been proof of the saying, "The road to hell is paved with good intentions!"? St. John of God, pray for me that I may follow my impulses to do good for others.

March 9 St. Frances of Rome (1384-1440) wanted to become a nun, but her family insisted that she marry. She would have liked to lead a quiet life, but she obeyed her mother-in-law's wishes and led a busy social life. She felt unhappy and alone, believing that no one understood her wish to do God's work on earth until she made the surprising discovery that her sister-in-law felt the same way she did. Finally, she had a companion who understood her love for God! The two young women set up a small chapel, sharing prayer time as well as doing what they could to help the poor. After she was widowed, St. Frances entered a convent that she had begun while still married.

St. Frances, you obeyed your family and your mother-in-law even though you wanted to walk a different path. Your friendship with your sister-in-law saved you from despair as the two of you shared a prayer life as well as giving charity to the poor. Do I have a friend who can share my path to Heaven and make my life on earth more meaningful? What work can we do together that would make this world a better place? St. Frances, pray for me.

March 10 St. John Ogilvie (1569-1615) was born in Scotland but, after he was ordained a Jesuit, was sent to France.

He begged to be sent back to Scotland where extensive massacres of Catholics were taking place. He wanted to do what he could to protect those who were faithful to the church despite threats of torture and death. Back in his native land, he escaped notice for 11 months after which he was caught and tortured in an attempt to get him to name the Catholics he served. He refused and went to his death without giving up one name.

What courage you showed, St. John. You were loyal, committed, and strong in your faith. What good qualities to imitate! I wonder if, seeing your steadfast trust in God, some of your captors became believers. We never truly know whom we have influenced, do we? Does my behavior always reflect my love for God and my fellow man as yours did. Who will be influenced by my behavior today? St. John, pray for me.

March 11 St. Constantine (died 337) was king of Cornwall. Legend has it that when his wife died, he gave his title and throne to his son and went to live in a monastery in Ireland. While there he did menial and basic tasks until he studied for the priesthood. He went to Scotland as a missionary and became an abbot. In his later years, while on a trip, he was attacked by pirates who cut off his right arm and he bled to death, making him Scotland's first martyr.

St. Constantine, you went from being a king to performing menial tasks by choice. There are many ways to serve God, and not all bring glory and status. God needs cleaners as well as preachers, cooks as well as kings. All work is good. Do I ever look down on some people's work because it is too degrading? Do I feel the work I do is more important than the work of others? Can I show respect to all who work, no matter what their jobs are? St. Constantine, pray for me.

March 12 St. Fina (Seraphina) (died 1253) did not have a long time to spend on this earth, but the time she spent was filled with love for God and with suffering. As a young child, she spent much of her time at home, helping her mother and praying. After her father died, St. Fina became paralyzed, unable to move from her place of rest, a wooden pallet she chose because it reminded her of the wood of the cross. When her mother died too, she had no one except one true friend. No one else would go near her because of the stench from her infected bedsores. St. Fina accepted her condition with resignation and never gave up hope that God would see her through her suffering.

St. Fina, it is hard to imagine what your life was like, six years lying on a wooden pallet, with no friends, not able to move about. You could have cursed your circumstances, but instead you accepted the life you were given without complaint. Everyone's life includes suffering, but those who have faith in God know that earthly suffering is nothing compared to the joys of an eternity with God. How do I deal with suffering? Do I accept my aches, pains, and illnesses and even welcome them as a way to share in the suffering of Jesus on the cross? Do I have faith that one day I will have no more suffering because I will be safe with my Father? St. Fina, pray for me.

March 13 Blessed Agnello of Pisa (1195-1236) was the founder of the English Franciscan Province by order of St. Francis. Along with eight companions, Agnello went to England without any money as is the Franciscan way. Their first winter was anything but easy as they had nothing to eat but bread and beer so thick it had to be watered down before they could drink it. Ignoring the harshness of their lives, they were so pious and cheerful that many were drawn to them.

Blessed Agnello, you were given a job by St. Francis and you did it cheerfully and with enthusiasm even though the conditions you lived under were harsh. You didn't complain or give up; you and your companions ignored hardship and got the job done. How often have I complained when something was not to my liking or given up on a job when I felt it was too hard? When was the last time I showed a spirit of perseverance in the face of difficulty? Blessed Agnello, pray for me. I want to be able to face difficulties with cheerfulness and enthusiasm like you.

March 14 St. Matilda (died 968) was the wife of King Henry of Germany. As queen, she lived a simple life, cared for the poor and prisoners, and founded several abbeys. She was well-loved. Unfortunately, when the king died, she made the mistake of putting one son, Henry, over another son, Otto, to inherit the throne and this favoritism led to warfare between the brothers and grief for St. Matilda. Before her death she spent years doing penance and performing works of charity.

St Matilda, your mistake was like that of Jacob who, in biblical times, favored Joseph over his brothers. Jealousy caused Joseph's brothers to sell him into slavery just as jealousy caused fighting between your two sons. Humans are not perfect and they make mistakes, but God forgives when they repent. Have I made any mistakes that I regret? Have I asked God's forgiveness and promised I would try not to make the same mistake again? St. Matilda, pray for me.

March 15 St. Louise de Marillac (1591-1660) met a priest, after her husband died, who was working with the poor and with orphans. Father Vincent, who later became St. Vincent de Paul, wanted to use peasant women as helpers instead of the aristocrats who helped him at the time believing that the poor would be better able to relate to them. St. Louise volunteered to organize and teach his new helpers. As the group of women she gathered grew in numbers, they became the Sisters of Charity, a religious community that today still cares for the poor, the aged, and orphans.

St. Louise, you remained faithful to your marriage vows until your husband's death. Then you pursued your dream of working for God. You were a very organized person. You found and trained the helpers Father Vincent needed, developing a community that still exists today doing charitable work among the poor. Sometimes I feel so disorganized both physically and mentally. What one thing can I do today to organize my mind, my work space, and my home? How can I schedule time for all I have to do including time for prayer? St. Louise, pray for me as I work toward a balanced, orderly life.

March 16 St. Abraham Kidunaja (6th century) was born in Mesopotamia to wealthy parents who arranged a proper

marriage for him. Instead of marrying, he ran off to the desert and became a hermit, living in a sealed hut. Friends gave him food and drink through a small opening. He left his cabin when he was asked to start a hermitage near Odessa where there were many pagans worshiping idols. St. Abraham suffered at the hands of the pagans especially after he destroyed their idols, but he persisted and eventually won them over to Christianity.

St. Abraham Kidunaja, you left your peaceful solitude for love of God. Despite persecution, you persisted in your mission to bring Jesus to the pagans. I have friends and acquaintances who are not believers. Do I ever bring God and his love up in conversation with them or do I not mention my beliefs because I am afraid of offending someone? Do I make excuses for not doing God's work on earth? God will help me find a way to introduce him to others if I just ask for his help. St. Abraham, pray for me.

March 17 St. Patrick (died c. 493) was not born in Ireland but he loved the Irish people and they loved him too. When he was a rather wild teenager, he was kidnapped and brought to Ireland to work as a slave. He regretted that he had not paid much attention to God and turned to him. When he managed to escape and leave Ireland, he became a priest and

my life? Do I share my beliefs for what He has prepared for me after this life is done? Starting today, can I look for opportunities to speak of him? St. Gabriel, pray for me.

March 25 Feast of the Annunciation is celebrated as the day when St. Gabriel the Archangel announced to Mary that she had been chosen by God to be the mother of the Christ Child. This announcement must surely have come as a great surprise to Mary. She was betrothed to Joseph and she must have believed that he would not marry her when he found out she was pregnant. Her entire life was to be changed, yet she agreed without hesitation to do the will of God.

Mary, my mother, you did not know where the path would lead if you agreed to bear the Saviour of the world. Yet, you did not question the angel; you simply said yes to God. How many times have I said no to God when He has shown me the way to do something for another of his children? Please pray for me that I may generously agree to do God's will no matter what the cost or how unclear the way.

March 26 St. Margaret of Clitherow (1555-1586) was married with two children, a Protestant in anti-Catholic England,

when she felt drawn to the Catholic faith. After converting, she began giving fugitive priests a safe place to hide from authorities. Her actions were discovered and she was arrested and sentenced to death if she would not renounce her faith. She refused and was put to death by crushing. Laid on a large rock, she was covered with a door loaded with heavy weights.

St. Margaret, you feared the pain that you faced, but you said your spirit rejoiced because you were able to remain true to your faith. What do I do when my faith is challenged by non-believers who, by a look or word, disparage my beliefs? How do I show my love for God and his church? Do I have the same courage you had, the same willingness to suffer for my beliefs? St. Margaret, pray for me.

March 27 St John of Egypt (died 394) became a hermit, living in a walled-up cell with only one window to the outside world. Although he scrupulously avoided contact with people, especially women as he feared temptation, this solitary life did not stop him from reaching out to the world. Every Sunday, huge crowds gathered to hear him preach through his little window. He also had the gift of prophesy and often foretold future events including military victories.

St. John, you used extreme measures to avoid

temptations. Temptation comes in many forms, through television, movies, ads, music of the day, or companions who have not been exposed to God's teachings. How good am I at resisting temptation? Do I think of God and my goal of living with him for eternity when temptation raises its head invitingly? Do I try to avoid places or people that might lead me away from God? St. John, pray for me that I may recognize temptation and resist it as you did.

March 28 St. Tutilo (born c. 850- 915) was talented as an architect, a painter, sculptor, poet, speaker, and metalworker. In fact, many of his works of art are to this day exhibited in European galleries and monasteries. After he was educated at a monastery in Switzerland, he decided to spend his life there as a monk teaching at the abbey school. He was not prideful about his many talents knowing they were gifts from God and did not seek fame, preferring the solitary and prayerful life of the monastery.

St. Tutilo, God gave you many talents and you used them to praise his name, never taking credit for his gifts. God is the source of any successes I may have. Do I give him not only thanks, but also recognition that, without him, I am nothing? Do I see God's hand in all I do and tell others how grateful I am to him for his gifts? What successes have I had lately that I can thank God for today? St. Tutilo, pray for me.

March 29 Sts. Gladys and Gwynllyw (died 500), according to legend, were married after St. Gladys' father refused to give St. Gwynllyw, a pagan, her hand in marriage. So, St. Gwynllyw kidnapped her. Various stories exist about this couple. Some say they both led a violent life engaging in banditry. Others hold that St. Gladys was always devoted to God and tempered the violence of her pagan husband. What is known is that, later in life, they lived separately as hermits, both examples of pious devotion.

God never gives up on any of us. That is what the story of your lives tells me, Saints Gladys and Gwynllyw. Whether you both led violent lives or whether you, St. Gladys, had to persist in bringing your husband to God, in the end you both became his faithful servants. Are there people I know, perhaps in my own family, whom I fear will never come to know and love God? Do I persist in my prayers for them and show, through gentle example, that God loves them and is waiting for them to come to him? Sts. Gladys and Gwynllyw, pray for me.

March 30 St. John Climacus (525-606) is also known as "John the Ladder" because he compared going to heaven to climbing a ladder with each rung more difficult to reach than the one before. His book, "The Ladder of Divine Ascent," describes 30 virtues, corresponding to the 30 years Jesus spent on earth before beginning his ministry, and how they can help humans rise to eternal life. St. John spent a great deal of time studying the lives of the saints and, although he was a hermit, helped the many people who went to him for spiritual guidance.

St. John, your visualization of our journey to heaven creates a very realistic picture in my mind. We make our way to eternal life step by step, doing our best to develop all the virtues we believe bring honor to God. Studying the lives of the saints, as you did, is a good way to learn about the virtues that will help us on our life journey. Can I make an effort to learn more about the saints so I can imitate their ways? Is there any saint whose life is most meaningful to me? Pray for me, St. John.

March 31 St. Benjamin (died c. 424) spent a year in prison because of his faith. He was released with the provision that he never speak of his faith to anyone again or he would face severe punishment. Threats could not stop this saint from

fulfilling what he felt was his mission on earth. He believed it was his obligation to let others share in the knowledge of God and he preached as often as he could. The threat against him was made good and he was again arrested and tortured in several horrible and painful ways until he died.

St. Benjamin, you knew that if you resumed your preaching, you would be put to death, but you did it anyway. Your mission was to spread God's word and that is exactly what you did. Isn't this the mission of everyone who believes in Christ's death and resurrection? Which of my friends or family members will I talk to about God? Who will I invite to come pray with me? Pray for me, St. Benjamin. I need courage to fulfill my mission.

+ April Opening Prayer +

As spring renews the earth, I renew my efforts to imitate you, the saints who won favor with God. *"The just man shall flourish like the palm tree; he shall grow like the cedar of Lebanon. They who are planted in the house of the Lord shall flourish in the courts of our God." Psalm 91:13-14*

April 1 St. Theodora (died 120) was in a good marriage, but she was tempted and committed adultery. Repenting, she dressed as a man and joined a monastery to make up for her sins. While at the monastery she was accused by a young woman of fathering her child. St. Theodora could have obviously proved that this was not the case but, instead, she accepted the blame and raised the little boy who later became the abbot of a monastery. Not until she died was it discovered

that she was a woman and therefore innocent.

St. Theodora, you were a sinner who repented and devoted your life to God. There is no sin that God cannot forgive; it is never too late for repentance. Just as Jesus was falsely accused and suffered in his innocence so you, too, did not deny the false accusation against you. False accusations can destroy a person's reputation. Have I ever falsely accused anyone or spread malicious gossip? Have I ever defended anyone falsely accused or refused to listen to gossip? The seventh commandment tells us not to bear false witness. St. Theodora, pray for me that I follow all God's commandments.

April 2 St. Francis of Paola (1416-1507) became a hermit when he was only 15 years old. When he left the hermitage, he and a few friends founded an order known as the Minim Friars emphasizing penance, charity, humility, fasting, and abstaining from meat. Later on in his life, he built a monastery on the site of his hermitage. He was a famous prophet and miracle-worker, so much so that the King of France wanted him at his bedside as he lay dying, hoping for a cure.

St. Francis did not cure the king but became life-long friends with his son, Charles VIII, who helped St. Francis build several more monasteries.

St. Francis, you were spiritual from an early age and your gift of prophesy and the miracles you performed made you famous, but did not make you proud. You spent most of your life in a monastery practicing what you preached: penance, charity, and humility. Do I ever make sacrifices as you did to do penance for my sins? Do I practice charity to those not as fortunate, giving of my time and treasure? Am I proud or do I humbly recognize that all my gifts come from God? Help me practice those virtues, St. Francis. Pray for me.

*April 3 **St. Agape (4th century)*** and her sisters, Chionia and Irene, were Christians living in Macedonia when it was against the law to own or have in your possession texts of Holy Scripture. The three women were convicted of owning texts and were told they must sacrifice to pagan gods. They refused and St. Agape and her sister Irene were put to death by being burned alive. Chionia was sent to a house of prostitution and later killed.

St. Agape, you studied the Word of God even though you were putting your life in danger every time you did so. Unlike you and others in repressed countries, I have the freedom to read holy scripture as often as I want. Do I take the time to read some verses of the Bible daily? Where can I put my Bible as a reminder to take a few minutes every day to turn to God's word for inspiration and spiritual help? Pray for me, St. Agape; I want to get closer to God through his words.

April 4 St. Isidore of Seville (560-636) was educated in the Cathedral School of Seville, under the tutelage of his rather harsh elder brother Leander and other learned educators. At one point, he ran away to escape the severity of his brother's stewardship but returned to become a brilliant scholar and a prolific writer penning a dictionary, an encyclopedia, a history of the Goths, and a history of the world among other things. In fact, all later histories of the Iberian Peninsula, Spain and Portugal, were based on his writings. He succeeded Leander as Archbishop of Seville and served in that position for 37 years rejecting dictatorial leadership and emphasizing democratic governing of the Spanish Church. St. Isidore of Seville is a Doctor of the Church.

St. Isidore, you leaned from the harshness of your early life that you wanted to rule democratically. Do I, whenever possible, at home, at work, or with friends, listen to the opinions of others or do I insist on having things my way? Do I believe that I know better than anyone else or do I acknowledge that other people have good ideas too? St. Isidore, pray for me. I want to value, as you did, the opinions and ideas of others.

April 5 St. Vincent Ferrer (1350-1419) served God as a priest and missionary during the time of a great schism in the Catholic Church when two men were claiming that they were the true pope, leader of the church. Although he tried his best, his efforts to heal the schism failed, and he searched for another way to serve God, eventually deciding the best way for him to serve would be to preach the gospel all over the world. Travel of any kind was very difficult at that time but, despite that, he preached and performed miracles in Spain, Germany, Flanders, Italy, England, Scotland, and Ireland and brought many new converts into the church. God granted him the blessing of living to see the end of the schism.

St. Vincent, you tried to be a peacemaker for God, but, when your efforts did not succeed, you took another avenue to serve him, and you worked hard to build up the church so when the schism ended it would be strong. When I fail to succeed at something on my first try, do I just give up or do I try to find another way to reach my goal? Do I give in to despair or do I trust that, with God at my side, anything is possible? God has confidence in me; shouldn't I have the same confidence? St Vincent, pray for me.

April 6 St. William of Eskilsoe (died 1203) went to Denmark to reform the monasteries there, probably chosen for this work because he had led a very holy and severe life as a priest. Unfortunately, the friars he was sent to reform had become very lax in their spiritual lives, and they did not want any part of reform. They persuaded the Danish nobles to join them as they opposed St. William and made his job very difficult. St. William never let the opposition influence him; he simply went ahead, did what he had been sent to do, and succeeded. He also became a prolific writer and his writings from that period are valued today as a history of Denmark for that period of time.

St. William, you had a job to do and you did it despite the fact that opposition made it difficult. Your sacrificial life, prayer, and giving up personal comforts made you strong so you could accomplish what you set out to do. It is hard to summon up courage when I am faced with opposition. Am I strong enough to do what I know is right even when I am criticized? Do I pray for the strength to be true to my convictions? Is there something hard that I must do right now that I need to give to God trusting He will give me all the help I need? Pray for me, St. William. I want to be a strong Christian.

April 7 St. John Baptist De La Salle (1651- 1719) life's work was to make sure the poor received an education and his actions are thought to have led to the institution of free elementary schools for all. The first step he took was to begin training young men to become teachers and this group, the Christian Brothers, became a teaching brotherhood with the men vowing that they would dedicate their lives to teaching the poor. At this period of history, education was only for the wealthy so of course this saint ran into a lot of opposition. Schools were attacked by those who felt that education for the poor should consist only of trade schools. St John led the way to teaching in the language of the country instead of Latin, using blackboards for instruction, separating students into classes based on their mental maturity, and providing education for all.

St. John, you knew that the best way to help the poor was to educate them, something unheard of in your time. Many people in the world today, even in our own country, do not get a good education. Buildings are substandard, books and other equipment outdated, and classrooms overcrowded. What can I do to help the situation? Do I know the issues and vote in school board elections? Do I make sure the children in my family are being well-served? Do I donate to charities that help provide education to children around the world? If I do any of these, I follow in your footsteps. St. John, pray for me.

April 8 St. Julie Billiart (1751-1816) was such a precocious child that, at age seven, she knew the catechism by heart and played school with her friends to help them learn it too. When she was 22 years old, an unknown person shot her father and St. Julie, as a result of nervous shock, became paralyzed from the waist down and spent the next 22 years in that condition, offering her suffering to God. Ignoring her own safety, she provided a hiding place for priests during the French Revolution and, disregarding her poor health, she nursed the wounded at the Battle of Waterloo. She also served as Mother General of the Sisters of Notre Dame de Namur, a teaching community she and a friend founded.

St. Julie, you did not let your disability stop you from accomplishing great things. You set your goals, offered your suffering to God, and let nothing stand in your way. You really believed that you could do anything with the help of God. What goals am I now trying to reach? Can I follow your example and trust in God to help me set reasonable goals and accomplish what I set out to do? Can I stop using excuses for not reaching my goals? Can I be more like you and refuse to let adversity get the best of me? St. Julie, pray for me.

April 9 St. Mary Cleophas (1st century) was one of the three Marys who were with Jesus at his crucifixion. She also went with Mary Magdalene to the tomb only to discover that Jesus was gone. There is very little more known of her life although some say that she went to Spain as a missionary.

St. Mary Cleophas, you were with Jesus when He was crucified, giving up his spirit to his father, and you were one of the women who discovered the empty tomb. Your sadness at his death must have turned into joy when you realized He had risen as He had said He would. Do I really believe with my whole heart and soul that Jesus died for me and rose from the dead to lead me to Heaven? You were privileged to know Jesus here on earth. Please pray for me that I may get to know him too one day and live with him for eternity.

April 10 St. Michael de Sanctis (1591-1625) was devoted to God from when he was a child and told his parents when he was only six years old that someday he would be a monk. When he was 12 years old, he asked to be admitted into

the monastery of the Trinitarians in Barcelona, Spain, and was later ordained a priest in a stricter order of the Trinitarians. Because of his great love for the Blessed Sacrament and his devotion to prayer and penance, he was already considered a saint by many while he was still living. After his death, many miracles were attributed to him.

St. Michael, some might ask why you were chosen as one of God's saints. You didn't found an order or do anything spectacular in your life. What you did is love God with a steady, unwavering love and you lived your life for him. Your life makes me realize that loving God and doing my best to be the person he wants me to be is my road to Heaven. Thank you for that lesson. St. Michael, pray for me.

April 11 St. Gemma Galgani (1878-1903) was drawn to prayer from a very early age. With both her parents dead, she was left at age 19 to care for seven brothers and sisters. When she was 20, she was stricken with meningitis, but she prayed to St. Gabriel of Our Lady of Sorrows and was cured. Although she wanted to become a nun, her application was rejected because the orders to which she had applied did not believe that she was fully cured. She offered this great disappointment up to God and she was honored to receive the wounds of Jesus on her

hands and feet every week for several years.

St. Gemma, your life was not an easy one. You raised your sisters and brothers, suffered with poor health, and were refused the one thing you wanted more than anything, to serve God as a nun. Yet all accounts of your life say that you always had a smile for everyone and God rewarded you with the honor of the stigmata. When things don't go my way, do I accept my disappointment with a smile realizing that God has other plans for me? What disappointment have I had in the past that turned out to be a blessing in retrospect? St. Gemma, pray for me.

April 12 St. Allerius (930-1050) never thought of becoming a religious until he came down with a serious illness. He then promised God that, if he were cured, he would become a monk. When he was well, he left his home in Salerno and entered a monastery in France. After he was ordered back to Salerno to work in the religious houses there, he withdrew to a hermitage outside that city. Many other hermits joined him and, together with twelve other men, he began the Benedictine Abbey of La Cava.

St. Allerius, you asked a favor of God and, in return, you were faithful to your promise to dedicate your life to him. How often have I asked for a favor? When the favor was granted, did I make some sacrifice to give thanks? I'm sure to thank friends for their gifts to me; do I extend the same courtesy to God? Is there some little sacrifice I can make right now to thank God for all He has given me? St Allerius, pray for me.

April 13 Pope St. Martin I (died 655) made an enemy of Emperor Constans when he refused to agree to one of the emperor's doctrines. The emperor sent an emissary to force all Italians to accept his doctrine, but Pope Martin refused. After a plan to assassinate the pope failed, the emperor forced him to go to Constantinople where he was brought before a court and accused of charges so ridiculous Pope St. Martin laughed at them. The pope continued to refuse to give in to the emperor and so he was exiled and imprisoned until he died.

Pope St. Martin, you had the courage of your convictions. No matter what the emperor did to you, you knew what you believed and you stood fast by those beliefs. I wonder if I know enough about what the church teaches to be as sure of my faith as you. How can I learn more about my church and its teachings? Reading the catechism of the church, attending classes, joining church groups that discuss the bible and how it relates to my faith: can I pick just one way to strengthen my faith? Pope St. Martin, pray for me.

April 14 St. Lydwine (1380-1433) suffered from many illnesses throughout her whole life. When she was about 16 years old, she broke a rib in a skating accident and never recovered from that fall. An abscess developed that burst causing great pain. She was subject to headaches, high fevers, muscle spasms, toothaches, blindness, and bouts of vomiting. God also honored her with the pain of the stigmata. She offered up her pain and suffering to God to make reparation for the sins of all people on earth.

St. Lydwine, it is hard to imagine all the illness you suffered and harder yet to know that you accepted that it was God's will and never complained. No wonder that you are considered the patron saint of those who are sick. Do I, like you, accept suffering and sickness and offer them up to God to show I am sorry for my sins? St. Lydwine, I ask you now to intercede with God for all my friends and family who are suffering, whether from physical, emotional, or mental causes.

April 15 Blessed Caesar de Bus (1544-1607) was uncertain about what he wanted to do with his life and, after trying his hand at writing plays, settled on a life in the military and at court. After he experienced firsthand the bloody realities of battles, he became ill and began rethinking his life, finally

turning to God and deciding to become a priest. He began his priesthood by teaching the catechism to poor families and, with his cousin, developed a program to further the goal of bringing knowledge of the church to all families. Out of this movement grew a religious order, the Fathers of Christian Doctrine.

Blessed Caesar, you saw a need in the church and you did your best to fill that need. If I were to look closely at our church today, would I see a need as you did? Can I make an effort to talk to my pastor and others in my church to see if there is a ministry that could use more help or have some need, however small, that I can fill? Is there anything that is keeping me from making a commitment to work for my church? Blessed Caesar, pray for me.

April 16 St. Bernadette (1844-1879) had a vision of a beautiful lady dressed in blue and white with stars around her head and roses at her feet. The Lady told her that she was the "Immaculate Conception" and that sick people who visited the site would be healed. At first, no one believed St. Bernadette's story. Then the Lady told Bernadette to dig, and a spring came out of ground. This and other miraculous happenings persuaded church authorities that the young girl was telling the truth. St. Bernadette entered a convent of the Sisters of Notre Dame and led a humble life of prayer until she died in 1879.

St. Bernadette, you were chosen by the Blessed Virgin to bring her message to the world. Despite facing doubt and ridicule, you did as she asked. Now, thanks to your courage and perseverance, many believers find peace and healing at Lourdes, the site of Our Lady's appearance. Am I brave like you, brave enough to stand firm in my beliefs so that I inspire others to have faith too? As long as I believe, as you did, that my treasure lies in heaven, I don't have to be afraid of anyone or anything on earth. Pray for me, St. Bernadette.

April 17 St. Robert of Chaise Dieu (died 1067) cared about the poor and, after becoming a priest, he founded a hospice for them. After living in Cluny for a while under the spiritual direction of St. Odilo, he felt called to give up his residence there and join forces with a fellow hermit settling down near Brioude, Auvergne. As other men followed and joined the two, St. Robert built an abbey, Casa Dei, for the growing community.

St. Robert, you attracted a large number of men who wanted to share a spiritual life with you. I think that believing in God and knowing you are doing your best to follow his commands gives one an aura of peace. Do people feel that aura about me? Does my love for God shine enough to attract others so they want to share what I have discovered through that love? St. Robert, pray for me. I want to be a spiritual magnet as you were.

April 18 St. Apollonius the Apologist (died 185) was a Roman senator who had converted to Christianity. One of his slaves reported his conversion to the emperor and he was arrested and told he must renounce his faith. When he refused, his case was brought before the senate and it was there that St Apollonius put forth a brilliant argument for being a Christian. Unfortunately, it didn't stop him from being condemned to death along with the slave who had denounced him.

St. Apollonius, you stated so well all the reasons why it makes sense to be a Christian. Even though your eloquent argument did not save you from death, it may have persuaded some who listened to you to believe in Christ. We never know what effect our words and action are having on people around us. Do my words and actions inspire faith in Christ? St. Apollonius, lend me some of your eloquence so I can influence others to love God too.

April 19 St. Timon (1ˢᵗ century) was one of seven men selected to serve as deacons to the apostles, helping them

spread the word of God. Acts, Chapter 6, verses 2 through 6 tells the story of how St. Timon was chosen as a man "of good reputation, full of the Spirit, and of wisdom." He became a bishop and was persecuted by the Jews and pagans because he preached the gospel. Thrown into a furnace, he emerged unharmed, but was later crucified.

St. Timon, you had the honor of being chosen to help the apostles in their God-given mission to spread his word. Despite persecution, you continued to preach the word of God even after escaping a fiery death. You had a job to do and you did it without complaint and without looking for recognition. Do I follow your example and do my work to the best of my ability in a way that pleases God? Do I worry about what others think of me or do I value God's opinion above all others? Can I offer up my daily work for God's glory? Pray for me, St. Timon.

April 20 St. Agnes of Montepulciano (1268-1317)

When St. Agnes was born, bright lights surrounded the house that was her birthplace, taken as a sign that this child was dedicated to God. She entered the convent at age nine, content to spend her days in prayer, but it seems God wanted her to serve in a different way. When she was only 14, she was asked to take over the time-consuming job of bursar, doing accounts and providing everything the nuns needed. The next year when she was 15, she was sent to be prioress of a convent and she obeyed. Later on in her life, she was needed to build a new convent and she again put aside her own desires and obeyed the will of God. No complaints were ever heard from this saint! St. Agnes has been the source of many miracles and was privileged to see the Blessed Mother and hold the Baby Jesus in a vision.

St. Agnes, you have shown us how we can obey God's will with good cheer. When my life takes a turn I don't like or I didn't plan for, do I sometimes become rebellious putting my selfish desires first? Do I complain or do I trust God wants the best for me and so look for the bright side of any situation? St. Agnes, pray for me that I may be more accepting of God's will and that I make the best of every circumstance of my life.

April 21 St. Anselm (1033-1109) was a Benedictine monk, a very kind and caring man, who served as the Archbishop of Canterbury, England. This famous Christian philosopher and theologian of the 11th century believed that it is not enough to merely accept the gift of faith. Instead, it is our duty to study and meditate on what our faith means to us so that we can truly understand this wonderful gift. He is best-known for his memorable argument for the existence of God.

St. Anselm, the world today is so busy that it's hard to find the time to sit quietly and reflect about what my faith means to me. My mind drifts to what needs to be done instead of staying focused. Yet, you are right. What use is my faith if I don't know what it means to me? When can I set aside some minutes each day to read and think about how faith influences my life and the life of those around me? When can I spend a few minutes of quiet time with my Lord today, clearing my mind of every thought, as I let his peace calm my spirit? St. Anselm, pray for me.

April 22 St. Tarbula (died 345), sister of St. Simeon, was consecrated as a virgin. Shapur, an anti-Christian king of Persia, falsely accused St. Tarbula of practicing witchcraft, causing his wife to suffer a serious illness. She was condemned to die along with several other Christian martyrs and was executed by being sawn in half.

St. Tarbula, your death was unjust and must have been excruciatingly painful. Keeping in mind the eternity you hoped to spend with God must have given you comfort while the executioners did their gruesome work. The promise of salvation sustained you through false accusations and unimaginable pain. Do I offer up, as you did, any pain or injustice done to me to God? Am I fair and just in my relationships so that I do not cause pain for others? Do I trust that God is with me always, that He is all the help I need, that eternity with him is worth any suffering I do here on earth? St. Tarbula, pray for me.

April 23 St. George (died c.304) is usually pictured battling with a dragon in order to rescue a young maiden. He was a soldier in the Roman army who rose to a high rank and was assigned as part of the personal guard to the Emperor. When he refused to take part in persecuting Christians, admitting that he himself was a Christian, he was condemned to death by beheading.

St. George, the dragon you are pictured slaying is a symbol of the evil in our lives that we must always be on guard against. It is not always easy to recognize evil as it comes in many shapes and forms. Sometimes it's the lazy way to do something without regard to whether it's the right thing to do, sometimes it's pleasure offered by friends, sometimes it's selfishness. Help me, St. George, to be on guard against the temptations that come my way every day. Help me fight my own personal dragons. Pray for me.

April 24 St. Fidelis of Sigmaringen (1577-1622) had two prayers he repeated over and over. He prayed that he might

never commit a mortal sin and he asked that he be allowed to die a martyr for Christ. This Capuchin priest preached against heretics not only in his sermons but in his many writings. He traveled extensively disregarding threats to his life and succeeded in converting and bringing many people back to the church. He was offered safety if he would renounce his faith, but he refused, accepting death instead.

St. Fidelis, your faith made you fearless in the face of physical suffering and you welcomed the opportunity to die for the faith you embraced. Do I fear rejection and disapproval if I take a stand on what I believe? Do I have the courage to speak out against practices that go against God's will, like TV shows extolling extramarital sex, jokes making fun of others, and songs that promote promiscuity? St. Fidelis, pray for me. I want to make a difference.

April 25 St. Mark the Evangelist (1st century) *who* was also known as John Mark wrote the second Gospel at the request of Romans who asked him to write about the teachings of St. Peter. He wrote it for the Gentiles who had converted to Christianity. Tradition has it that St. Mark traveled with St. Peter, St. Paul, and his cousin, St. Barnabas, as what we would call today a go-fer, a person who had assorted duties to make it easier for the apostles to spread the good news.

St. Mark, you played an important role in helping the apostles teach the Gentiles about God. Your humility in accepting and doing work that enabled them to evangelize is an example to me that whatever good work I do does not have to be recognized here on earth. What little thing can I do today to make this world a better place? Can I do it without looking for praise and recognition? St. Mark, pray for me.

April 26 St. Pedro de San Jose Betancur (1626-1667) is known as the "St. Francis of the Americas." Born to a poor family in the Canary Islands, he migrated to Guatemala when he was 24 hoping to find work with a relative there. He was so destitute when he arrived that he joined a bread line run by the Franciscans and decided that he would like to become a priest. He tried very hard at his studies but was not successful at mastering the material, so he joined the secular Franciscan Order and began working with the poor and destitute in Guatemala. He was responsible for opening a hospital, shelters, and a school for the poor. His work with the poor attracted other young men who wanted to help too and so, with them, he started the Bethlehemite Congregation.

St. Pedro, you were not able to follow your dream of becoming a priest, but you didn't let that stop you from dedicating your life to helping the poor. God does not always answer our prayers in the way we would like, but He always answers them in the way that is best for us. Have I been disappointed in a response to a prayer? Do I see any reason for my prayer not being answered in the way I wanted? Do I trust that God knows what he is doing and that his answer to all my prayers is the best one for me? St. Pedro, pray for me.

April 27 St. Peter Armengol (1238-1304) was born to a noble Catalonian family but was living a life of corruption as a bandit when he came face to face with his father who was part of a group of men sent to rid the area of criminals. Immediately he put down his weapons, asked forgiveness, and swore to change his life. He became a friar and devoted his life to saving people who were being held hostage by the Moors, making two trips from Spain to Africa to redeem captives. At one point he was captured and hanged, but was rescued by a fellow missioner.

St. Peter Armengol, you turned your life around when you realized the error of your ways. You asked forgiveness for what you had done and went on to lead a good life. God forgives us anything as long as we repent and make amends. Am I in any situation now that is causing me to sin? Do I want to walk away from this temptation? How can I do that? St.

Peter, help me recognize sinful occasions and pray for me that I have the strength to walk away from them.

April 28 St. Louis Mary de Montfort (1673-1716) was a very popular preacher whose missions attracted thousands of people and brought many into the church. He loved Our Blessed Mother very much and he wanted everyone to love her as he did, especially urging all to imitate Mary's acceptance of God's will revealed in her words to the Angel Gabriel, "Behold the handmaid of the Lord; be it done to me according to thy word." He founded the Missionaries of the Company of Mary for priests and brothers and another organization, the Daughters of Wisdom, to serve and care for the sick.

St. Louis, Our Blessed Mother was very important to you and you wanted everybody to share in the special feeling you had for her. The Mother of God is our mother too and she deserves honor and respect and love. When she was asked to be the mother of God, she never hesitated but said yes to God. Do I accept God's will for my life as she did? Can I say a Hail Mary right now and spend a few minutes in conversation with her? St. Louis, pray for me. I want to show my devotion to Our Heavenly Mother as you did.

April 29 St. Catherine of Siena 1347-1380) had a vision, when she was a child, of Jesus saying, "Please give me your heart." From that day on, she dedicated herself to him and eventually became a Dominican nun. St. Catherine was bold in speaking out to rulers, popes, or other famous people when she felt her advice would do some good. She persuaded Pope Gregory XI to return to his place of residence in Rome from France where he was in exile. During the Great Western Schism when an anti-pope was gaining support, she wrote letters to church and state leaders championing Pope Urban VI and denouncing the anti-pope.

St. Catherine, your letters made a difference in your world and our church. You didn't care about what anyone thought of you; you did whatever it was you believed was right. Do I do the same? When someone, stranger or friend, uses God's name in vain, do I explain that it offends me? Do I speak up and protest when I see someone doing something that is mean or cruel? Can I write letters to the newspapers about current events that affect issues of my faith? I want to be brave like you. St. Catherine, pray for me.

April 30 Pope St. Pius V (1504-1572) was a leader who recognized that the Catholic Church needed reforming and, when he was elected pope, he did just that. He issued the

Roman Catechism and the Roman Missal. He strengthened the Church by having the decrees of the Council of Trent published in all countries where there were Catholics and making sure they were followed. The Council of Trent clarified Catholic doctrine on salvation and the sacraments and standardized the Catholic Mass.

Pope St. Pius V, you acted as guardian of the church, introducing needed reforms and making sure the changes were followed. Our church has not always been perfect; leaders who forgot their mission on earth led the faithful away from God's laws. You recognized and successfully addressed a need in the church. Am I a watchful member of our church? Do I keep informed about what is happening in the church today? Are there any needs in my church community that I can help with right now? Pope St. Pius V, pray for me.

+ May Opening Prayer +

Our Blessed Mother, whom we honor during this month of May, I know you smile upon my efforts to imitate the saints. Please give me clarity of mind and purpose so that I can follow the path they have marked for me, the path that leads to eternal life. *Holy Mary, Mother of God, pray for us sinners, now and at the hour of our death. Amen.*

May 1 St. Peregrine (1265-1345) was the ringleader of rebels who, when they were young men, opposed the Pope, and he struck the Pope's ambassador who had been sent to seek peace. Regretting his action immediately, he asked for and was granted forgiveness. To make up for his past, he joined the Servites and gave his life to the poor and sickly. People who have cancer often pray to this saint because a cancer on his foot was completely healed after the saint dreamed that Christ had touched it.

St. Peregrine, you chose a path that was not pleasing to God when you led the rebels who opposed the Pope and attacked his ambassador. When you realized that what you had done was wrong, you humbled yourself to ask forgiveness and spent your life doing penance for your sins. Is there anyone whom I may have injured in some way whose forgiveness I should seek? What is holding me back from doing that before any more time passes? Is there anyone who has hurt me whom I can forgive as the Pope forgave you? St. Peregrine, pray for me.

May 2 St. Athanasius (296-373) vowed, as bishop of Alexandria, to continue the fight of his predecessor against a heresy in the church, Arianism, which claimed that Jesus was not divine. His dedication to eradicating Arianism caused him to be exiled five times for a total of seventeen years away from Alexandria and his flock. He never swerved from the path he felt he had to take to protect the church and its doctrines and his writings carried on the battle against Arianism.

St. Athanasius, you never gave up the fight against those who preached false doctrines even though it cost you great sacrifice and separation from your home. You were a true defender of the faith. When I meet people who are ready to put down my beliefs, do I follow your example and defend my faith no matter what it costs me? Do I know enough to show others how their ideas about my faith may be wrong? Do I ask the Holy Spirit to give me wisdom in choosing the words I say? St. Athanasius, pray for me.

May 3 Saints Philip and James (Ist century) never looked for recognition for their work so there is not a lot known about them. James the Less, the younger of the two apostles called James, may have been a cousin of Jesus. He was a deacon taking care of logistics like food and lodging for the apostles. He became bishop of Rome and was stoned to death. St. Philip is mentioned in several places in the New Testament and seems to have been a very down-to-earth person. It is Philip who asked Jesus to let the apostles see the Father so they might know him. Jesus replied that since Philip had seen him, he had seen the Father. The relics of both these saints are together in Rome.

Saints Philip and James, you were content to do God's work on earth without a sense of your own importance. You did whatever needed doing without asking for fame or fortune. We all like to be recognized for our good deeds, especially when they involve some sacrifice on our part. Do I always need to be praised for what I do or can I be satisfied knowing that God sees everything? Where can I be more humble in my service to others or to God? What good can I do today in a quiet, unassuming way? Saints Philip and James, pray for me.

May 4 Blessed Carthusian Martyrs (died 1540) refused to swear to the Oath of Supremacy instituted by King Henry VIII. This oath stated that the king was the supreme head of state and church, denying the pope's authority. The king wanted this group of monks to swear the oath because they were so highly regarded, and he believed their support would give legitimacy to his divorce and remarriage. Eighteen refused, resulting in some being hung, drawn, and quartered while others were thrown into prison, chained, and allowed to starve to death.

Blessed Carthusian Martyrs, you would not deny that the pope, the successor of St. Peter to whom Jesus entrusted his flock, is the head of the church. There are many different ways of worshipping God, but I feel so fortunate that I can trace my church back to its founder, Jesus Christ, and our first earthly leader, St. Peter. Do I ever think to thank God for this privilege He has given me? Blessed Martyrs, pray for me that I never turn my back on this gift from God.

◇< ◇< ◇<

May 5 St. Angelo (2nd century) and his twin brother were born to Jewish parents who converted to Christianity. Both boys were very intelligent, speaking Latin, Greek, and Hebrew, and were very spiritual. St. Angelo became one of the first members of the Carmelite Order along with his twin when they were 18 years old. After living five years as a hermit, St. Angelo went to Sicily where his powerful preaching and numerous miracles converted many to the faith. A man whose wickedness St. Angelo had denounced sent a gang of men to stab him to death. Like Jesus, this saint forgave his murderers and prayed for them even as he lay dying.

St. Angelo, you forgave your killers and prayed for them that they might repent and be saved. When someone feels hurt, it's hard to put bitter thoughts aside and forgive. You followed Jesus' example even though no greater wrong could have been done you. Is there anyone against whom I hold a grudge, someone who has hurt me whom I am slow to forgive? Can I put aside my hurt feelings and anger and say a prayer for anyone who has harmed me? St. Angelo, pray for me.

May 6 Blessed Edward Jones (died 1590) was born an Anglican in Wales and educated in Rheims. He converted to Catholicism, became a priest in 1588, and was sent to serve in England. England at that time was ruled by Elizabeth I who was purging the country of the Catholicism established during

the reign of her predecessor, Queen Mary, a devout Catholic. After two years, Edward was arrested and, under severe torture, admitted that he had renounced his Anglican faith and had become a priest, acts that were considered treason under Elizabeth. He gave an eloquent argument at his trial that confessions elicited through torture should not be admitted into court. Despite this, he was condemned to death and hanged, drawn, and quartered.

Blessed Edward Jones, you argued at your trial that confessions elicited by force are not grounds for conviction. The court praised your courage but still held you guilty of treason and condemned you to death. Your plea for justice went unheard. There are so many places in the world today where justice is an unknown word and torture is commonplace. The people of those countries need prayers. Do I pray for them? Do I always act justly? Blessed Edward, pray for me.

May 7 Blessed Rose (1656-1728) was engaged to be married, but when her fiancé died she decided to enter a convent and then left that haven when her mother was widowed. As she cared for her mother, she organized a group of woman who met to recite the rosary together. Realizing how little these young people knew about God, she and a friend

opened a free girls' school and began to train others to teach. Some people, at that time, did not believe in education for women and harassed her and her helpers, but they ignored the opposition and organized many schools throughout all of Italy. The group of women she organized became the Venerini Sisters who, today, work with Italian immigrants in the United States and other countries.

Blessed Rose, you were a dedicated teacher who was responsible for bringing the knowledge of God to many young women. Despite harassment, you carried out God's commands to carry his message to the world. How am I spreading his word? We teach in many ways, not just in classrooms. We teach by our actions and our words. Are my actions and words teaching others about God's love for all people? Can I become more conscious of how I act and speak so I never lead anyone away from God? Blessed Rose, pray for me.

May 8 St. Magdalen of Canossa (1774-1835) had a very unhappy childhood. Her father died when she was two and when she was five, her mother left her and her four brothers and sisters in the care of an old uncle. St. Magdalen spent eight years under the tutelage of a governess who disliked her immensely and she suffered several illnesses that almost led to

her death. Asking God what she was to do with her life, she was shown that the poor and suffering needed her help. She immediately began reaching out to the poor, educating them in academic subjects as well as knowledge and love of God. She founded the Institution of the Daughters of Charity to carry on her work.

St. Magdalen, instead of feeling self-pity and cursing God for all the sorrow and pain in your own life, you asked him how you might best serve him. You accepted your suffering while finding a way to do his will. Do I accept suffering or do I complain when I am sick or face disappointment? Do I think of suffering as a way to make my faith stronger? What pain am I suffering now that I can offer to God? St. Magdalen, pray for me.

May 9 St. Pachomius (292-346) was taken into custody by the Roman army against his will and held in captivity when he was just 20 years old. Christians who lived in the area where he was imprisoned brought food to the prisoners and tried to comfort them. The actions of these good people so impressed St. Pachomius that, when he was freed, he was baptized and went on to begin a new form of monasticism, one where monks lived together in a community instead of in solitary cells.

Your story, St. Pachomius, makes me wonder what influence my actions have on those around me. The good Christians converted you, not with words, but with their kindness and generosity. Am I a kind and generous person? Does what I do bring people to God or does it lead them away from him? Realizing that my actions may be having a great influence on someone in my life, what kind or generous action can I take today? St. Pachomius, pray for me.

May 10 St. Damien of Molokai (1840-1889) was ordained a priest and left his homeland of Belgium to work for ten years in Hawaii as a missionary. He then felt a call to serve the lepers who were exiled to Kalaupapa, an isolated peninsula on the island of Molokai. He was able to minister to these neglected men and women for 16 years before he contracted the disease.

St. Damien, with no thought to your own safety, you went to live among the lepers, people who had been abandoned by the world. It must have been a great comfort to them knowing that there was someone who loved them enough to put his own life in harm's way. You followed the example of Jesus when He showed his love by dying on the cross for our sins. There are many lonely and sick people who have no one to visit them and show them compassion and love. Is there a neighbor, fellow parishioner, or acquaintance whose loneliness and pain I can ease? Can I make the time to offer them my friendship? St. Damien, pray for me that I might become a source of comfort too.

May 11 St. Odilo of Cluny (962-1049) was a great promoter of the "Truce of God" and was known as the "Archangel of Monks." After the collapse of the Carolingian Empire in the ninth century, France had separated into many small lordships and counties and there was a lot of fighting. The church, in order to bring peace though nonviolent means, instituted the "Truce of God," a time when all military actions were stopped for religious reasons, when sanctuary was guaranteed to all who took shelter in a church, and when people had an opportunity to live for a time in peace. St. Odilo also served as the Abbot of Cluny, France, for 53 years, during which time he reformed monastic rules and supervised the rapid growth of the number of monasteries in Europe.

St. Odilo, you worked for peace. All people deserve to live in peace without fear that their loved ones, homes, and personal safety are threatened. We need peace in our world today. What can I do to help bring peace to the world? There is a hymn that says "Let peace begin with me." Am I, in my own little world, a peacemaker? Do I do my best to resolve quarrels, control anger, and pray for peace? St. Odilo, pray for me.

May 12 St. Dominic de la Calzada (died 1039) was a hermit whose most remembered work was that of rebuilding an old Roman road complete with a stone bridge so that pilgrims might visit the shrine of Santiago de Compostela in Spain more easily. He also used an old palace as a hospital to give aid to pilgrims on the way to the shrine. This building was renovated in 1965 to be used as a parador or hotel. A town grew up around St. Dominic's hermitage and was named after him. A "calzada" is a road and thus the name given to this holy hermit.

St. Dominic, you made the traveling of pilgrims easier with your work restoring the road to the shrine. We are all on a journey that will ultimately bring us to God. How can I make the road easier to travel for everyone I know? How can I help my loved ones along the way as you did? St. Dominic, help me as I travel to eternity. Pray for me.

May 13 Our Lady of Fatima (appearance1917) appeared to three young children in Fatima, Portugal, six times between May 13th and October 13, 1917. At this time in history when World War I was such a bloody disaster, she promised that the whole world would be at peace if people listened to her and followed her requests. Our Lady of Fatima said that we must pray the rosary for the conversion of Russia or that country would cause wars and persecutions against the church. Countries that survived the destruction would be ruled by atheistic Russia. Her message had three parts. The first part gave a picture of what the fires of hell are like, World War II was foretold in the second part, and the third part had to do with dangers to people of faith.

Our Lady came to earth to warn and to counsel the world through the three youngsters she chose to carry her message. Just as she predicted, wars seem to be erupting all over this earth and we see more and more disparaging remarks and actions being taken against people of faith. Am I listening to her message and saying the rosary each day for peace in the world and in my church? Do I pray for the conversion of the Russian people? When would be the best time for me to spend some time obeying Our Lady's wishes? Our Lady of Fatima, pray for me and for world peace.

May 14 St. Matthias (1ˢᵗ century) was not one of the original apostles, the twelve chosen by Jesus, but he was devoted to Jesus and had followed him from the time of his baptism. After Jesus ascended into heaven, the apostles gathered to choose a replacement for Judas. It was important that the apostles number twelve because that was the number of the tribes of Israel. It was also important that the new apostle be someone who had been faithful to Jesus through all the good and bad times and who could give witness to the resurrection. St. Matthias was chosen.

St. Matthias, you were a loyal follower of Jesus even though you were not one of the chosen twelve. It was enough for you to be one of the seventy disciples who served him from his baptism by John through his ascension into heaven. We are all chosen to serve God in some way. Do I look for opportunities to serve him? How can I serve God today? How can I, through a word, a smile, or a friendly action, show Jesus' love to someone? St. Matthias, pray for me.

May 15 St Isidore (Ysidro) (1070-1130) worked on farm near Madrid as hired hand for the DeVargas family. Every day on the way to work he stopped at a shrine to attend Mass making him late for work. The other workers complained, so Juan DeVargas decided to see whether this was true. The

employer observed that, even though Isidore did come to work late each day, he did twice as much work as the other workers, so Isidore was allowed to continue attending Mass. St. Isidore, who always prayed as he worked, had a great reverence for animals and he helped the poor. He and his wife, St. Mary de la Cabeza, are proof that ordinary people, like you and me, can become saints in Heaven.

St. Isidore, you were an ordinary person like me who worked hard to earn a living for your family. You put your heart into your work giving over one hundred percent but you didn't ignore your obligation to serve God. You attended mass and helped those who were poorer than you. Am I keeping the parts of my life in balance as well as you? Do I make time for God, for my family, for my work, and for myself? Do I give my best in everything I do? St. Isidore, pray for me.

May 16 St. Brendan of Clonfert (c.460-577) and his monks traveled to a wonderful "Land of Promise," overcoming sea monsters, flaming rocks, and other frightening obstacles. This legend about the saint is the reason he is often asked to keep travelers safe. St. Brendan was a monk who founded monastic communities in Ireland and throughout Europe, monasteries that were centers of art and learning where monks

made beautiful copies of old Roman and Greek manuscripts. The monastic life was not easy. Most days were spent in long hours of silence and prayer, food was sparse, and, lacking the comfort of a bed, monks slept on the hard floors of their cells.

St. Brendan, you spent your whole life spreading the word of God while you gave up most of life's comforts. The life you and your monks lived was harsh, yet beautiful manuscripts came out of that austerity. No matter what happens to me, whether I suffer physical, emotional, or mental anguish, God is just a breath away if I only look for him. Where do I see proof of God's presence in my life? Is there some way I can share my faith with someone I know whose eyes are shut to the beauty of God's world? Who can I help? What can I say? St. Brendan, pray for me.

May 17 *Ascension of the Lord* is celebrated on this day, forty days after Easter Sunday. In some dioceses this day is a holy day of obligation, but in many the feast is celebrated on the following Sunday. "Now he led them out towards Bethany, and he lifted up his hands and blessed them. And it came to pass as he blessed them, that he parted from them and was carried up into heaven." St. Luke 24:50-51.

How can we not believe in heaven when so many witnesses tell us that Jesus was crucified, rose from the dead, and then left the earth to ascend into heaven? Doubts can't take root in my soul if I remember those three facts as recorded in the gospels of Matthew, Mark, Luke, and John. Jesus, from your home in heaven, pray for me that I never doubt your life and death were gifts to me from God the Father so that I might spend eternity with you.

May 18 Pope St. John 1 *(died 526)* was supreme pontiff when the Catholic Church was split into the eastern and the western churches. The emperor of Rome sent him to Constantinople, now Istanbul, to make peace with the Eastern Church. Pope St. John was greeted with great enthusiasm in Constantinople because this was the first visit a pope had made to that region. He was successful in bringing unity between the churches, but when he returned to Rome, the emperor was displeased with the agreement and threw Pope St. John into prison where he was allowed to starve to death.

Pope St. John, you were a peace-maker. We need more people like you in our world today because peace seems as if it will never come. What can I do to make this a more peaceful world? Do I pray continually for peace? Have I made peace with my family and friends by forgiving any wrongs done me? I can let peace begin with me, with every word I say, with every action I take, starting now. Pope St. John, pray for me.

May 19 St. Celestine (died 432) was pope for four months when he decided to give up his position and throw himself at the feet of the Cardinals humbly begging forgiveness for not being able to govern successfully. His peaceful, gentle spirit made it impossible for him to be an effective church head. For most of his life he was a hermit who stayed busy reading, writing, and doing manual labor so the devil would not find him idle and tempt him.

St. Celestine, your humility in admitting that you were not an effective leader is a good example for me. God gives everyone different talents. There are many things in this world that others do better than I, but there are things that God has given me the talent to do. Am I humble enough to admit I need help when there is something I don't have the knowledge or aptitude to do? Do I humbly offer my help to others when I see they need a helping hand? St. Celestine, pray for me.

May 20 St. Bernardine of Siena (1380-1444) volunteered to work at a large hospital in Siena during an outbreak of plague in 1400 taking care of victims until he fell ill himself, an illness from which he never completely recovered. He worked with such enthusiasm that he persuaded other young men to help too. He went on to care for a dying relative for over a year, again putting his all into his work. He was ordained a Franciscan and, after several years of living a quiet life, began to preach. As usual, he put everything he had into his preaching and drew so many to the church that Pope Pius II called him the "second Paul." If you have seen in church the letters IHS, a monogram for the name of Jesus, surrounded by a sun symbol, you have seen the sign that St. Bernardine used to promote devotion to the name of Jesus.

St. Bernardine, whatever you did, you gave one hundred percent. You were never lukewarm, whether the task was one that drew public notice or one that was done in the quiet of your home. Do I do my work, whether at home or out in the world, with as much gusto as you or am I a lukewarm worker? Do I offer all my work up to God? Am I eager to serve God by doing my best? Pray for me, St. Bernardine.

St. Mary Magdalene, in your humility, you gave thanks to God for his gifts knowing that you had not earned them. I have done nothing to earn the gifts God has given me either. How am I using the special gifts that God, through his goodness and love, has given me? What kind act can I perform today to show I am grateful for his never-ending love and gifts? St. Mary Magdalene de Pazzi, pray for me.

May 26 St. Philip Neri (1515-1595) was a cheerful man who found that humor was a good way to practice humility. He was a humble man himself and often asked others to do something ridiculous to humble themselves like singing a funeral song at a wedding or wearing a hair shirt over one's clothing, actions which would cause others to laugh at them. As a layman, he founded a society of people who wanted to help the sick and the poor. He went to Rome and, entering the priesthood there, became known as one who could tell penitents their sins before they confessed them and who heard confessions hour after hour. He never stopped helping others and believed that "Cheerfulness strengthens the heart and makes us persevere in a good life."

St Philip Neri, you were always helping others in some way with a cheerful spirit and true humility. You remind me that showing joy and cheer is a sign that God is with me. Do I always do what needs to be done with joy and good will? Do I try to keep a happy heart and smile more frequently than I frown? Do I try to bring joy to others around me? St. Philip Neri, pray for me.

May 27 St. Augustine of Canterbury (died c. 605) set out from Rome with 40 monks to evangelize England, but turned back when he heard rumors of how terrifying the Celts were. Pope Gregory the Great reassured him that he had nothing to fear and that this was a job he must do. St. Augustine mustered up his courage and led his group back to England where they converted the king, founded a See in Canterbury, and had success in spreading the faith.

St. Augustine, you were afraid to lead your group to England, but you pushed aside your fears and got the job done. So many times I am afraid as you were, and troublesome questions plague me. What lies ahead? What path should I choose? Am I doing the right thing? As Pope Gregory assured you that, with God, you had nothing to fear, I am reassured that God knows my fears and is waiting to help me if I just ask and trust in his answer. St. Augustine, pray for me.

May 28 St. Mary Ann of Jesus of Parades (1614-1645) was born in Quito, Ecuador, the youngest of eight children. She led a very quiet life, but her 31 years on this earth were filled with closeness to God and a spirit of service to God's people. As a secular Franciscan, she lived at home with her parents and only went out to go to church or to perform some act of charity. In her city of Quito, she established a clinic and a school for Africans and indigenous Americans and nursed residents who were brought down by the plague. Whenever she was needed by others, she didn't hesitate to help whether it was for an earthquake or an epidemic.

St. Mary Ann, you lived a quiet life but you were always there when anyone needed you. You gave of yourself and trusted that God would help you help others. How willing am I to help others when they are needy? Do I give of myself with trust that God is my helper if I am doing his work? Do I know someone right now who could use my help and my prayers? What am I doing about it? St. Mary Ann, pray for me. I want to be a willing helper to God's people.

May 29 St. John de Atares (died 750) was a hermit in the Pyrenees whose home was under a rock promontory.

Saints Votus and Felix, brothers, joined him to live as hermits too. In later years, the Benedictine monastery of St. John de Ia Pena was built on the site of their hermitage. We celebrate the lives of all three men on this day.

Sts. John, Votus, and Felix, you spent your lives meditating and praying. So often we think that we have to be busy every minute to be useful. How soothing and peaceful it would be to take some time for just being with God, talking to him, and getting to know him. The greatest gift we can give anyone, God and ourselves included, is our time. Do I take a "break" from the stress of each day to sit quietly and refresh my soul with my Savior? Do I give God and myself time together each day so we can become closer? Good saints, pray for me.

May 30 St. Joan of Arc (1412-1431) was a young shepherdess when she heard St. Michael the Archangel and other saints telling her to fight against the British in order to restore the French Dauphin to power. She led the French army to victory and crowned Charles VII King of France at his palace at Rheims. In 1431 she was betrayed and fell into the hands of the English; she was held in prison for a year while church interrogators, politically motivated, tried to find reasons to execute her. Finally, because she would not deny that she had heard heavenly voices, she was burned

at the stake as a heretic. She was only 19 at the time of her death.

St. Joan of Arc, you were tried, convicted, and killed because you would not deny that the voices you heard came from God. Everyone turned their backs on you. Even the Dauphin whom you restored to power did not try to help you. When friends fall away, especially in time of need, it is good to remember that our one true friend, Jesus Christ, will always be by our side, loving us and helping us in all our troubles. St. Joan of Arc, pray for me.

May 31 Feast of the Visitation is the day we celebrate Mary's visit to her cousin Elizabeth who would in a few months time give birth to St. John the Baptist. "Now in those days Mary arose and went with haste into the hill country to a town of Juda. And she entered the house of Zachary and saluted Elizabeth. And it came to pass that, when Elizabeth heard the greeting of Mary, the babe in her womb leapt. And Elizabeth was filled with the Holy Spirit and cried out in a loud voice saying, 'Blessed art thou among women and blessed is the fruit of thy womb.'" St. Luke, 1:39-42

Blessed Virgin Mary, when you heard your cousin was pregnant after many years of not being able to conceive, you

137

hurried to her side and helped her through the last three months of her pregnancy. You yourself were carrying the son of God, yet you didn't hesitate to serve Elizabeth. You accepted your exalted position as a gift from God without false pride. Do I understand, as you did, that all I have comes from God? Do I believe that my talents and my treasures are gifts from him or do I think that I have earned them in some way? If I believe that all I have is due to God's love for me, not because of something I have done, then I will never be guilty of false pride. Mary, my mother, pray for me.

+June Opening Prayer+

Help me, God, as I continue learning about the holy saints, to imitate their attributes so that I too may bring glory to your name and, one day, live with you for eternity.

"Save us, O Lord, our God, and gather us from among the nations that we may praise thy holy name and may glory in thy praise." Psalms105:47.

June 1 St. Justin (d.165) was one of the first Christian philosophers. Starting early in life, he read the works of poets, historians, and orators searching for the truth of God. When he was 30 years old, he found what he was looking for in the scriptures and became a Christian. He was an "apologist," using his philosophical and writing skills to argue with pagans who misunderstood and attacked the

church. He was beheaded in Rome for his beliefs.

St. Justin, you used all your skills defending the church against misunderstandings and attacks. The unknown is scary to people; I think that is why many people attack our faith. What can I do to help others understand my faith better? Do I show by my actions that I expect others to respect my faith and do I show respect for their beliefs in return? When someone tells me a joke or story that is derogatory to any religious belief, do I let them know that I don't care to hear anything that makes fun of a religious faith or practice or do I laugh because it's easier? St. Justin, pray for me.

June 2 Sts. Marcellinus and Peter (d.304) were secretly condemned to die during the persecutions of Diocletian. St. Marcellinus, a priest, and St. Peter, an exorcist, a person authorized by the Church to work with those possessed by demons, were led into the woods for the execution so no one would know where they were buried. Legend says that, when they were told they would be beheaded, they, with good cheer, began to clear the place where they would be laid to rest.

Saints Marcellinus and Peter, you did not fear death but went toward it cheerfully because your faith assured you that you would soon be with God. Leaving this earth is such a mysterious journey but, if we have lived our life walking in God's path, won't that path lead straight to him? What are my thoughts about death? Am I afraid or do I look forward to finally seeing the face of God? Am I doing everything I can to make sure I spend eternity in heaven? Holy Saints Marcellinus and Peter, pray for me.

June 3 St. Charles Lwanga and Companions (d.1886) lived at the court of King Mwanga of Uganda, a pagan and cruel pedophile who forced young boys and men to submit to him. St. Charles Lwanga and his companions not only refused to give homage to pagan gods, they also protected each other from the king's homosexual demands. When the king demanded that they either give up Christianity or be put to death, they chose death and were either killed on the way to the place of execution or burned to death.

St. Charles Lwanga and companions, you showed great bravery in the face of death. You protected many young boys from a depraved king and you didn't renounce your beliefs. Preying on young children sexually is a terrible thing. What can I do to help protect young children in my family and neighborhood? Have I seen any commercials, TV shows, or movies that cast children in a sexual light? If my answer is "yes," can I protest against them by writing a letter to the producers? Pray for me, brave saints of Uganda, and for all children who are being exploited.

June 4 St. Optatus (died 387) worked hard to bring unity in the church. During the persecutions of the emperor Diocletian, some clergy renounced their faith out of fear. When the persecutions ended, these men repented and returned to the church. A group of church members called Donatists believed that these clergy should not be welcomed back and allowed to practice as clergy. St. Optatus argued in their behalf and he succeeded in preventing a schism.

St. Optatus, you wrote many treatises to keep our church united under one pope. There are so many examples of disunity in our world today. Followers of dissimilar political parties and religions look at their differences rather than the ways they are alike. We need unity more than ever. How can I promote unity? Am I willing to listen to the ideas of others and discuss them without anger? Do I share my beliefs without trying to force them on anyone else? St. Optatus, pray for me. I want to be a unifier like you.

June 5 St. Boniface (672-754) set out to convert the Germanic tribes to Christianity and used an unorthodox way to get

their attention. There was a huge oak tree called "Thor's Oak,' dedicated to the god Thor. St. Boniface chopped it down calling upon Thor to strike him down for attacking his holy tree. Of course, Thor could not harm him and this bold action converted many Germans. A fir tree growing up on the same spot gave St. Boniface the opportunity to compare Christ, our everlasting light, with the fir tree that remains green even in the dark days of winter. Legend says this was the first Christmas tree.

St. Boniface, like Jesus the greatest teacher of all, you brought converts into the church using hands-on examples. Your missionary work brought about the birth of Christianity in Germany. We are all called to be missionaries, telling others of Christ and his love for us. Where can I preach God's word? What tangible examples can I use to show how much he loves us? Pray for me, St. Boniface, that I recognize and seize any opportunity to share my faith in a clear and loving way.

June 6 St. Norbert (1080-1134) went from the luxuries of a noble family to a pleasure-seeking life at court without giving much thought to his soul. Once, when on a trip, he ran into a severe storm and a bolt of lightning caused his horse to bolt, throwing St. Norbert to the ground where he lay for an hour. Just as St. Paul did when awakening on the road to Damascus, St. Norbert asked God what

He wanted him to do. He felt God's answer, "Go and do good. Turn away from evil." St. Norbert gave up his position at court, became a priest, and gave away all his possessions.

St. Norbert, you changed your life after asking God what He wanted from you. What, I wonder, does God want from me? Have I asked him for direction? Have I asked him to lead me to the path He wants me to follow? Are there paths I'm following now that He might want me to change? St. Norbert, pray for me as I search for God's purpose for me in this life.

June 7 St. Gottschalk *(died 1066)* was a Christian prince until his father was murdered. Then he renounced his faith and, vowing revenge, gathered an army which was defeated. He was thrown into prison and his land given away. When he was released, he went to Denmark and fought in that country's wars before moving to England. He married there and returned to the faith. In time he regained control of his lands and princely title and worked to organize the Slavic people into a Christian kingdom.

St. Gottschalk, you were so angry at your father's death that you turned your back on God and looked for revenge. Your time away from God was not a good time for you. It was not until you returned to your faith that your life turned around for the better. I know many people who have fallen away from God. Do I try, through loving words and actions, to help them realize that loving God and following his commands is the only way to a full life? Do I invite them to share spiritual opportunities? St. Gottschalk, pray for me and for all who are refusing to accept God's love.

June 8 St. William of York (died 1154) was elected Archbishop of York in 1140, but he was accused of simony (the buying or selling of a church office) and being unchaste. He was shown to be innocent of all charges by Rome, but, with the advent of a new pope, the charges were brought again and St. William was relieved of his duties. He went to Winchester and lived as a monk until another pope ascended the chair of Peter and reinstated St. William as archbishop.

St. William, false accusations hurt your good name and caused you to lose your position as Archbishop of York. In any age false accusations as well as gossip and telling lies about others can cause a lot of damage. Have I ever been guilty of spreading malicious gossip, or accusing someone without any foundation for my accusation, or of telling lies? If I have, I am sorry, and I will guard my tongue so it doesn't harm anyone ever again. St. William, pray for me.

June 9 St. Ephrem (306-373) was born into a Christian family in Mesopotamia. He was both a teacher and a deacon of the church. When Christians in Persia were being persecuted, he left that land and finally settled in Edessa. While he was living in Edessa, a famine occurred and St. Ephrem heard that some people were hoarding food. He persuaded them to let him distribute the food fairly among everyone. St. Ephrem spent the last years of his life as a hermit, writing songs, poems, and commentaries of the bible to counteract the heresies that were flourishing in the church at that time. He left us a legacy of hundreds of songs and poems about the faith.

St. Ephrem, you used your musical and writing talent to instruct people about God and to stop the heresies that were dividing the church. Many of our modern day hymns are based on verses from the bible so singing hymns to God is not only a beautiful way to praise him, it is also an opportunity to learn something of Holy Scripture. Do I always sing during church services? Could I join my voice with others more often to shout his glory? Do I listen to the words as I sing and think about their meaning? St. Ephrem, pray for me.

June 10 St. Landericus (died c. 661) was the Bishop of Paris. During a famine, he first sold off all his possessions to

help the poor. When that wasn't enough, he then sold church belongings. He worried that the care given to the poor was substandard as it depended on the generosity of donors. With that in mind, he started Paris' first hospital to care for physical needs of the poor and also welcomed the Benedictines into his diocese to see to their spiritual needs.

St. Landericus, you were wise to provide for your people both physically and spiritually. It's hard to concentrate on God if you're hungry and homeless. There are many poor and homeless today who need help. How can I continue your work in my own small way? Is there some organization that I can help financially? Can I volunteer to work in a shelter or a charity that provides food and clothing to the poor? Guide my steps, St. Landericus, and pray for me.

June 11 St. Barnabas (d. 61) became a Christian in the year 30, then sold his land and gave the money he received to the Apostles. For the rest of his life, he worked with the Apostles helping to manage the money they collected for those suffering from famine in Jerusalem and spreading the word of Jesus. It was Barnabas who convinced the Apostles to forgive St. Paul his former persecution of Christians and to open their hearts and preach, not only to the Jews, but also to the Gentiles

who had come to believe in Jesus.

St. Barnabas, you believed that people are capable of becoming more Christ-like if they come to know and love God. You saw the good in St. Paul and in the Gentiles who, through acceptance of the words Jesus preached, changed and became his followers. Do I condemn those who have fallen away from God or do I believe they can change and come to know and love him? Do I pray for and try to help them so they can turn toward God again? Is there anyone I know right now who needs my prayers? St. Barnabas, pray for me.

June 12 Pope St. Leo III (d.816) was named pope on the same day that his predecessor died. The Emperor Charlemagne of France, whom St. Leo regarded as a protector of the Holy See, gave him a share of his captured riches which St. Leo used to help churches and charities. In a plot to remove this saint from office, he was beaten and his attackers tried to tear out his eyes and his tongue. The saint was rescued and miraculously recovered. Charlemagne escorted him back to Rome to assume his papal duties and ordered the attackers put to death. St. Leo pleaded for their lives and, instead, they were exiled for life.

Pope St. Leo III, you were viciously attacked but, instead of wanting revenge, you showed mercy for your attackers.

There are people in the world today hurting innocent people for misguided reasons of revenge, hatred, or learned ideology. It's hard to forgive terrorists who rejoice when they kill innocent people, but, if we are to follow Christ's example, that is exactly what we must do. Can I forget my anger and pray that God will change their hearts? Pope St. Leo, pray for me, for all the innocents who have been killed, and for those who, as Jesus said, "Know not what they do."

June 13 Saint Anthony of Padua (1195-1231) is most famous as the saint to turn to when searching for lost articles. Few realize that this Franciscan friar was also known as the "Wonder Worker" because his preaching was so effective that it made people from all roads of life turn from sin. For a time, his superiors thought he would not make a good preacher so he was never asked to give sermons. One day, however, a speech was scheduled for an important meeting and there was no one to give it except St. Anthony. He gave an impromptu sermon and his powerful oratory astounded the audience. After that, St. Francis himself told St. Anthony that he was to preach and teach theology which is what he did until his death at age 36.

St. Anthony, I have come to you many times for help when I have lost something and you haven't let me down. You prepared yourself for God's call by studying God's word, and, when the time came to use your talent and knowledge, you were ready. Am I prepared to do God's work? Do I understand my faith well enough to explain it to someone else? St. Anthony, please pray for me that when I am called on to do something for my Lord, I will be ready too.

June 14 St. Joseph the Hymnographer (died c. 886) was born in Sicily but had to leave his home when it was invaded by Arabs. He settled in Constantinople for several years but left to escape persecution. On his way to Rome, he was captured by pirates and held as a slave. When he escaped, he returned to Constantinople and founded a monastery there. He was a very productive hymn writer, credited with composing over 1000 canons.

St. Joseph, you had to leave two homes for fear of persecution and then spent years as a slave, but none of your troubles dimmed the music in your heart. You raised your voice to God in praise and left your music for others to use in praising God too. Do I use my voice during church services to give thanksgiving to God and to show him how much I love him? Do I offer my very voice to God so that I never say anything that will cause others to fall way from his love? St. Joseph, pray for me.

June 15 St. Germaine Cousin (1579-1601) lived a life of severe emotional and physical abuse at the hands of her stepmother who despised the fact that St. Germaine was a sickly child born with a deformed right hand. She was denied food, had boiling water thrown on her legs, and had to sleep in the barn with the sheep. She was given the job of caring for the sheep and, after slipping off to mass each morning, spent her days praying with a rosary made of knotted string. Her prayers were that she would please God and her stepmother whom she forgave.

St. Germaine, the story of the abuse you suffered brings tears to my eyes. I cry for you and all the abused people in the world today. Have I ever seen signs of someone being abused and ignored it because I didn't want to get involved? Do I know how to report signs of abuse? Do I pray for abused people whether children or adults and donate to or help at shelters for the abused? St. Germaine, pray for me and for all who are facing abuse of any kind.

June 16 St. John Francis Regis (1597-1640) was a spiritual person from his very young years. He became a Jesuit and was sent to be a missionary in several parts of France where the people had strayed from the faith during a long

period of civil and religious troubles. He was not a flowery speaker but his simple sermons and plain words brought many back to God. His help for the poor included organizing hostels for prostitutes and helping girls from the country avoid the life of prostitution by establishing them in lace making and embroidery work.

St. John Francis Regis, you helped people in so many ways. Your simple sermons and concern for the poor brought many people back to God. Your work with young girls kept many from a life of prostitution. You looked around you and tried to fix what you saw needed fixing. What in my world needs fixing now? Do I see a need I can address? Is there someone in my life who could use a helping hand right now? What stops me from reaching out to them? St. John Francis, pray for me that I might have the courage to make this a better world in any way I can.

June 17 St. Emily de Vialar (1797-1856) was born after the French Revolution when a wave of anti-church feelings swept over the country. Her baptism and the family's practice of religion had to be done in secret. When she was 15, her mother died and she became housekeeper for her father, but they became estranged when she refused to marry.

When her grandfather left her a sizeable inheritance, she founded the Congregation of Sisters of St. Joseph of the Apparition in Gaillac, France, to help the poor and sick. The community suffered after much of her inheritance was lost because of a poor money-manager. Despite her financial problems and suffering for many years with a hernia, she helped her community grow from one house to 40.

St. Emily, you had a mission to help the sick and to educate children. No matter what setbacks you had, you kept your eye on your vision and succeeded in what you set out to do. How can I imitate you? I have good intentions, but as the saying goes, "The road to hell is paved with good intentions." How can I transform my intentions to visit a shut-in, to help a friend in some way or even just to read a book to a child into reality? Can I set one goal to do something kind today and make sure I follow through? St. Emily, pray for me.

June 18 St. Gregory Barbarigo (1625-1697) agreed to interview a daughter of a friend who wanted to study at the University of Padua where he was chancellor. Although it was unheard of at that time for women to attend university, the saint was so impressed with the young lady, Elena Coanaro, that, despite strong disapproval of the faculty, he agreed to

have her become the first woman to attend the University of Padua. She was such a talented student that faculty members vied to honor her at her graduation.

St. Gregory Barbarigo, even though many women today are free to pursue whatever field of study interests them, there are too many places in the world where women are mistreated and kept from developing their minds. I thank you for having the wisdom to allow a woman of your time to study and learn, and I thank God for allowing me to be born in a place where the right of everyone to study and learn is honored. I will pray that people everywhere recognize the value and rights of women as you did. St. Gregory, pray for me and for oppressed women everywhere.

June 19 St. Romuald (950-1027) spent his youth more interested in worldly things than in religion. When he was 20 years old, he went to a duel where he saw his father kill his opponent. This so horrified the young man that he fled to a monastery where, after much hesitation, he became a monk. He felt beset by temptations and led a very severe life, giving much of his time to establishing monasteries all over Italy.

St. Romuald, seeing your father kill a man influenced the rest of your life. You felt you had to make reparation for what he did and you spent your life devoted to doing God's work. Is there ever a reason to take another's life? How do I feel about capital punishment: is it a fitting sentence or is it revenge? How do I work against abortion and euthanasia: with my votes, with my work for pro-life organizations, with my donations? St. Romuald, pray for me, that I never lose sight of how precious God's gift of life is.

June 20 Blessed John Fenwick, John Gavan, and Anthony Turner (died 1679) were Jesuits who were martyred after being falsely accused of being part of the Titus Oates Plot. A man by that name said Catholics were plotting to kill Charles II, replace him with his Catholic brother, James, and then murder all Protestants. There was no such plot except in the mind of the story's creator, but, nevertheless, sentiment against Catholics ran high and many were put to death simply because they were Catholics.

You holy men were the victims of discrimination against Catholics. Discrimination is wrong no matter who it targets. God made everyone on earth; we are all brothers and sisters no matter what our color, our race, our ethnicity, or our religious beliefs. Do I laugh at jokes that put down another religion or race? Do I harbor biased thoughts about others who are not like me? Blessed martyrs, pray for me, that I never, even when joking, show discrimination against any of God's children.

June 21 St. Aloysius Gonzaga (1568-1591) was born into a noble Spanish family, but he gave up his inheritance to become a priest. He began theological studies having already shown that he had a gift for both philosophy and theology. In the fourth year of his studies, a plague broke out in Italy. Putting aside concern for his own safety and disregarding the fact that his health was not the best, St. Aloysius cared for the sick until he contracted the disease himself and died.

St. Aloysius, you had a brilliant future ahead of you as a Jesuit, yet you gave it all up to tend to the plague-stricken people of Rome. Your actions illustrate the words of Jesus: "Love your neighbor as yourself." Do I always put myself first? Have I ever put aside concern for myself to help someone else? Do I know of anyone right now who could use my help even if giving that help inconveniences me? With your help and prayers, I will try to be less selfish and think about others' needs as well as my own. St. Aloysius, pray for me.

June 22 St. Thomas More (1478-1535) was a lawyer who lived for at time at a Carthusian monastery. Leaving the monastery, he married and entered politics, ending up in Parliament. King Henry VIII made him Lord Chancellor but he resigned this position when the king's view of marriage and supremacy of the pope conflicted with his own. He spent the rest of his life writing about the church. When he refused to give allegiance to the king as head of the Church of England, he was imprisoned, tried, found guilty of treason, and beheaded.

St. Thomas, you were a staunch Catholic, and King Henry's wishes to legitimatize his marriages and to usurp the pope's authority went against all you believed. You gave up a high position in government in peaceful protest. God wants us to obey civil authority, but, when I believe our leaders are acting unjustly, do I take a stand? Do I use peaceful means to protest injustices? St. Thomas, pray for me. I want to make my voice heard in a way that is pleasing to God.

June 23 St. Joseph Cafasso (1811-1860) was born with a deformed spine and was handicapped all his life. As an ordained a priest, one of his most important missions in life was to advocate for prisoners. He worked to improve prison conditions and cared

for condemned prisoners, even accompanying them to the gallows. His kindness won many prisoners over to the church and many were baptized just before being put to death.

St. Joseph, you worked in a ministry that many people shy away from. It can be frightening to visit prisons, but so worthwhile when you can turn a life around and bring it to God. If my church has a ministry for visiting prisons, is that something I feel I can do? Is there a local branch of Dismas House, the organization that helps released prisoners rehabilitate? Could I help there in some way? St. Joseph, pray for me and for all those who are imprisoned today.

June 24 St. John the Baptist (1ˢᵗ Century), the second cousin of Jesus, was born six months before Our Savior. His parents, Zachary and Elizabeth, had prayed for a child. The Angel Gabriel appeared to Zachary and told him their prayers would be answered with a child to be named John for he would be the one to proclaim the Christ Child. Fulfilling this prophecy, John preached by the Jordan River, baptizing Jesus and his followers. After Salome danced for King Herod, the king told her he would give her any gift she desired. Her mother told her to ask for the head of John the Baptist.

St. John, you baptized many in the name of Jesus Christ

and even baptized Christ himself. In Baptism all our sins are wiped away including original sin and we are left with a clean slate, but our human inclination to sin is not wiped away. Am I aware of people, places, and things that might lead me to sin? Do I make a conscious effort to avoid them? Is there anything or anyone in my life right now that is tempting me to sin? St. John, pray for me. I want to offer Jesus a pure soul.

June 25 St. William of Vercelli (1085-1142) was a hermit who settled at Monte Vergine, Italy. He was soon joined by many others who were attracted by his holiness and the miracles he performed, including restoring the sight of a blind man. A church was built in honor of Our Blessed Mother and St. William became the abbot of the religious community called the Hermits of Monte Vergine. Unfortunately the monks under St. William complained that his rule was too strict so he moved on and founded several other hermitages across Italy.

St. William, you founded several hermitages and you enforced strict rules at each one. Sacrifice was your way of honoring God. Your miracle of restoring sight to a blind man makes me wonder about how much I see or pay attention to in the world around me. Am I so wrapped up in myself that I see injustice and ignore it? Do I see unkindness and look the other way? St. William, help me to see and do something about the wrongs I witness. Pray for me.

June 26 St. Maxentius (died 515) was a monk who left his monastery for a period of about two years, not because he had lost his faith. No, what he was trying to do was escape from the fame that had surrounded him because of the many miracles he had performed. When he finally returned to the monastic life at St. Maixent, he was elected abbot and, when the abbey was threatened by soldiers, he miraculously saved it.

St. Maxentius, in your humility, you did not want the fame that your miracles brought you. Everything we do comes from God. He was the source of your ability and you did not want to take the credit that was rightly his. Do I always believe that God is behind everything I do or do I claim sole credit for my successes? Am I humble and thankful to him or am I filled with false pride? St. Maxentius, pray for me that I may always recognize God's hand in my life.

June 27 St. Cyril of Alexandria (ca. 376-444) rose to Mary's defense when Nestorius, the patriarch of Constantinople, preached that she could not be called the

mother of God because he did not believe that Jesus was both divine and human. St. Cyril, who was the patriarch of Alexandria, succeeded in having Nestorius and his teachings condemned. St. Cyril wrote many articles about the Incarnation and the Trinity that helped stop the spread of the false beliefs about Mary. Because of this saint we can say, "Holy Mary, Mother of God, pray for us sinners now and at the hour of our death."

St. Cyril, you defended Mary's status as the mother of God. Many people think that Mary is not an important figure in the story of Jesus, but we know that, as his mother, she deserves our utmost respect and devotion. How can I get closer to Mary, my mother, and the mother of our Lord, Jesus Christ? Can I say at least one decade of the rosary, her special prayer, every day? Can I use her and her willingness to accept God's will as my model? St. Cyril, pray for me. Help me give our Blessed Virgin Mary the place she deserves in my life.

June 28 St. Irenaeus (c. 125-c.202) became the Bishop of Lyons after the previous Bishop was killed by persecutors. While he was Bishop, a heresy called Gnosticism grew in Gaul. Putting it simply, Gnosticism was based on the belief that we are saved not by faith and works but by knowledge and those

who had knowledge were superior to those who did not have it. St. Irenaeus wrote down all the beliefs of the Gnostics and contrasted them with the teachings of the apostles. His writings laid the foundations of Christian theology and helped bring an end to Gnosticism.

Saint Irenaeus, you refuted the Gnostic heresy very logically by writing a comparison between false and true beliefs. Do I really believe that Jesus lived and died for ME? Do I believe that He rose again and went to prepare a place for ME? Do I believe that God wants everyone on earth to share eternity with him? Do I shore up my faith with good works? St. Irenaeus, pray for me. I do not ever want to be led astray by false teachings.

June 29 Sts. Peter and Paul (1ˢᵗ century) Saul of Tarsus hated Jesus and persecuted Christians. One day, on the road to Damascus, he was knocked off his horse by something like a lightning bolt. It was then he began to believe in Jesus; he was baptized and his name was changed to Paul. He started new Christian communities and traveled from place to place preaching about Jesus. He is considered by some to be the greatest missionary of the New Testament period.

St Peter was a Galilean fisherman, married, and a brother

of St. Andrew. His name was actually Simon, but Jesus named him Peter when He asked him to head his church. "Thou art Peter and upon this rock I will build my church." Peter committed a very human sin in denying Jesus three times at the time of the crucifixion, but Jesus never doubted Peter's love for him.

Saints Peter and Paul, you both sometimes did things that one would not expect of a saintly person. Your lives show us that God loves us despite our human natures and forgives all our sins as long as we repent. Is there any sin that sits heavy on my soul now that I should confess? Can I take it to God now knowing He will forgive me anything? St. Peter and St. Paul, pray for me.

June 30 First Martyrs of the Church of Rome (1ˢᵗ century) were blamed by Nero, the fifth and final emperor of the Julio-Claudian Dynasty, for a crime many believed he himself had committed. In AD 64, the city of Rome went up in flames and burned for six days and seven nights. Nero was quick to put the blame on the Christians of Rome. They were rounded up and martyred, with some fed to wild dogs and some covered by pitch and wax and set alight on stakes.

You were the first martyrs of the Roman church, giving

your lives because you proclaimed your belief in Jesus and his teachings. You showed us, by your courage and steadfastness, that, under no circumstances must we deny God. Do I remain silent when others speak disparagingly of my faith? Do I try to explain my faith to friends who have mistaken beliefs? How far out of my comfort zone am I willing to go to show my love for God? Holy martyrs, pray for me.

+July Opening Prayer+

God, I know that you see everything I do, and you see into my heart and know the reasons for my actions. By imitating your holy people, I hope to please you. *"God looks from heaven upon the children of men to see whether there is anyone who knows and seeks God." Psalm 52:3.*

July 1 Blessed Junipero Serra (1713-1784) taught philosophy and theology at the University of Padua after being ordained a Franciscan. He volunteered to cross the ocean and work in the Mexican territory of California taking over the Jesuit missions that had been abandoned when the Jesuits were forced to leave. He founded 9 missions and converted thousands of Indians, teaching them not only about God but about farming, ranching, and arts and crafts. He was a tireless

worker and is credited with the spread of the church on the west coast of the United States.

Blessed Junipero Serra, you volunteered to leave your comfortable life and travel to a distant land to spread God's word. Your concern was not just for the souls of the natives, but for their quality of life. You showed us that if we are to truly help the needy, we have to consider all aspects of their lives. Do I donate to food and clothing drives generously? Are there programs in my city that help adults learn to read or learn a craft where I could offer my services? Am I doing all I can to show God's love to the poor? Blessed Junipero Serra, pray for me.

July 2 St. Oliver Plunkett (1625-1681) was the last Catholic martyr to die in England. Born in Ireland, he was ordained a priest in Rome and, because of persecutions, could not return to Ireland. When he was named Archbishop of Armagh and Primate of Ireland, he did return and worked very diligently building up the church by establishing schools, ordaining priests, and confirming many. Then, in 1673, the persecutions started again and, determined not to leave his people, he went into hiding until he felt it was safe to work openly. Unfortunately the persecutions intensified and, in 1679, he was falsely charged of treason and, after the Irish government could not convict him, he

was tried in an English court. Not having time to bring his witnesses to England, he was found guilty and sentenced to hang.

St. Oliver, you cared for the Irish people so much that you would not leave them even though it was dangerous for you to continue your work in Ireland. Today there are many people who are being persecuted for their religious beliefs just as you were. Who is caring for them? Who is bringing their cause before people who could make a difference? Our missionaries need our prayers and donations. Am I doing all I can in those areas? St. Oliver, pray for me.

July 3 St. Thomas the Apostle (1st century) is best remembered because he is the apostle who doubted that Jesus had risen from the dead until he was able to touch his wounds. He was a missionary in Persia and India although initially he was reluctant to travel to those countries. In fact he had to be taken there as a slave by a merchant who was traveling that way. Set free, he began his work and founded many churches and converted so many that some believers in that part of the world still call themselves "Christians of St. Thomas."

St. Thomas, once you had proof that Jesus had risen, you gave him your whole heart. You were afraid to take up your missionary work, but, again, once you were put in place, you gave

167

your all. Sometimes I, like you, am reluctant and afraid to share God's words with others. What can I do to get over this shyness, to get started sharing my faith? Can I share a story about how prayer has helped me in some way? Can I tell about the peace I feel when I am conversing with God? St. Thomas, pray for me.

July 4 St. Elizabeth of Portugal (1271-1336) became queen of Portugal at 12 years of age with her marriage to King Diniz, an amoral man who abused her and engaged in many illicit affairs. Despite her suffering, she prayed for her husband who converted later in life. She had two children, a son and a daughter. Her son, jealous of the favors given to his father's illegitimate children, brought his forces into battle with those of his father. St. Elizabeth rode out onto the battlefield, stopped the fighting, and helped the two reconcile their differences. She brought about peace one other time when her son was waging war against his son-in-law, again riding out onto a battlefield to help them reconcile.

St. Elizabeth, you were a brave woman and a peacemaker. You dared to intervene in disputes that were tearing your family and your country apart. We need peace in this world of ours and the peace has to begin within our families. Are there members of my family who are harboring grudges against each other? Is there anything I can do to bring the individuals together? Can I forgive anyone in my family who has hurt me in some way? St. Elizabeth, pray for me.

July 5 St. Anthony Mary Zaccaria (1502-1539) had a successful career as a medical doctor but felt there was something lacking in his life. After spending a great deal of time studying the life of St. Paul, he felt called to the church so he could bring others to Jesus as St. Paul had done. He gave his inheritance to his mother, became a catechist, and was ordained a priest. He founded a group called the Clerks Regular of St. Paul or Barnabites for men religious and the Angelics of St. Paul for uncloistered nuns. The men and women in these orders encourage frequent reception of the Blessed Sacrament and cooperative work between lay people and religious.

St. Anthony Mary, you encouraged lay people to work with religious to further the work of the church. There are many opportunities in my church for people like me to contribute. How can I find out where help is needed? What ministry calls to me as you were called? Can I be an usher or lector, wash and iron altar linens, sing in a choir, teach children in religious education? Surely there is something I can do to work with the religious in my church. When will I offer my services? St. Anthony Mary, pray for me.

July 6 St. Maria Goretti (1890-1902), the patron saint of youth, was born in Italy in 1890. When she was nine years old, her father died and, along with the other family members, she had to work hard on the family's farm. When Maria was 11 years old, a neighbor boy, Alexander, made advances to her and, although she kept refusing, he would not give up. Becoming angry at her persistent refusal, he attacked her with a knife and mortally wounded her. Dying in the hospital, she forgave him and prayed he would go to heaven someday. In later years he repented and became a Capuchin brother.

St. Maria Goretti, you refused to give up your purity even in the face of death, and you showed your understanding of Jesus' love for others by forgiving the one who attacked you. The world today seems to be so accepting of immoral actions, even to the point of admiring and imitating those who are most sinful. How can I be pure of heart and avoid temptation? How can I influence others, especially young people, so they do not look up to those who seem to have forgotten God? Can I refuse to watch movies or TV shows that glorify immorality? Can I let local stations know that some of the shows they air are not decent? St. Maria Goretti, pray for me.

July 7 St. Astius (died 117) was a bishop in Macedonia during the reign of Emperor Trajan, a fanatical persecutor of Christians. The saint may not have been surprised when he was imprisoned and crucified because he had had a dream about suffering and dying for the faith. Before he died he was smeared with honey and laid out for hornets to attack. A group of his friends were put to death too, simply because they sympathized with him.

St. Astius, you dreamed that you would someday die for the faith and you did not back away from the future you saw. I don't know what my future holds, but I hope I can be as strong a Christian as you and your friends were. Can I accept, without complaint as you did, any pain I suffer whether it's physical or emotional? Can I offer my suffering up to God? St. Astius, pray for me.

July 8 St. Morwenna (5th century) built a church for the local people in Cornwall with her own hands, carrying the rocks on her head from beneath a cliff. Where she stopped to rest, a spring gushed out of the ground that can still be seen today near the church. The daughter of a king of Wales, she is one of several Welsh saints who moved to Cornwall. She made her home in a small hermitage at the top of a hill that

overlooked a wild and stormy part of the Atlantic Ocean from which, on certain days, she could see her native land. When she was on her deathbed, she asked that she be propped up so she could see Wales one more time.

St. Morwenna, you struggled physically to build a church for the people who lived near you, rock by rock. How am I helping to build my church? Do I invite a friend who has shown interest in my faith to attend services with me? Do I talk about my faith? Do I live it as God wants me to so I can be an example to others? St. Morwenna, pray for me. I want to help build my church too.

July 9 St. Augustine Zhao Rong and Companions (17th-20th centuries) were martyred at various times between 1648 and 1930. They varied in age from nine years old to over 70. Many were Chinese lay people; others were priests and nuns. Augustine Zhao Rong was a Chinese soldier who became a priest. He was martyred in 1815. The practice of Christianity has always been difficult in China; at times Christians were allowed to practice freely and at other times were driven underground. These martyrs chose to practice their religion despite persecution and possible death.

Over a span of four centuries, you martyrs kept

Christianity alive in China even when facing persecution and death. How much your faith must have meant to you! How seriously do I take my faith? Do I take it for granted because I am free to worship as I wish? Do I value it above everything else in my life? Is Jesus my most precious treasure? If I believe that, how do I show it? Blessed Saints, pray for me.

July 10 St. Veronica Giuliani (1660-1727) was a practical woman. Although she received the stigmata and had many ecstatic visions, she performed her duties matter-of-factly as novice mistress and then abbess of a Capuchin convent and brought about needed improvements like a new water system. To make sure there was no fraud involved when she received the stigmata and when an imprint of the crown of thorns appeared on her head, the bishop put her under observation for a long period of time until he determined that there was no trickery involved.

St. Veronica, it seems you had two lives. One was your closeness to Jesus as you shared the pain of his crucifixion and the other where you did your work with common sense and practicality. Your heart was with Jesus, but your feet were planted firmly on the ground. Do I keep God close to me as I go about my work by offering prayers throughout the day? Do I do my best for God and for those I serve here on earth? St. Veronica, pray for me.

July 11 St. Benedict (480-543) wrote a Rule for his order of monks that was so strict an attempt was made to poison him! He was born into a noble Roman family, the twin of St. Scholastica. Because he felt that Rome was a wicked place, he ran away and lived in the mountains outside of the city. For three years he lived alone in a cave, some say fed only by a raven. As young men heard of the life Benedict was leading, they came and asked to stay with him; this was the beginning of the Benedictine Order. St Benedict founded 12 monasteries in all and is credited with many miracles. His motto was "Pray and work."

St. Benedict, you felt it was best to avoid temptation and left Rome rather than be led into sin. There are so many temptations today that surround me, but I cannot physically leave my home. What temptations are calling to me now? Do I do my best to turn my back on them? Am I a good example to others who want to avoid sin too? St. Benedict, pray for me.

July 12 St. John Gaulbert (died 1073) wanted revenge on the person who murdered his brother. He met him in a place

where the man had no way to escape, drew his sword, and would have killed him but the man begged for his life in the name of the passion of Jesus. Immediately, St. John put aside his sword and embraced his enemy. After this incident, St. John became a Benedictine monk and humbly refused all requests to be abbot. Instead, seeking solitude, he and two companions built a small monastery. Later St. John went on to found several other monasteries.

St. John, you wanted revenge, but your enemy's pleas touched your heart and you forgave him. His prayers also brought you back to the service of God. Prayers are powerful. Isn't it said that they can move mountains? Do I pray for those whom I don't care for as well as my friends and family? If I pray for terrorists and world leaders who want to destroy innocent people, will it touch their cold hearts? St. John, pray for me.

July 13 St. Henry (972-1024) was a German king and Holy Roman Emperor. Both he and his wife, St. Cunegunda, were spiritual and prayerful people. St. Henry cared for his world and tried to make it a better place by working to reform the church, building schools, and putting down rebellions while trying establish peace in Europe. Beginning with a battle with his brother who challenged his position, King Henry was drawn

into many wars, reluctantly at times, but he always treated those he defeated with mercy and kindness.

St. Henry, you ruled with an iron fist and a charitable heart. You cared about making this world a better place and you succeeded in doing just that even when you had to go to war to do so. There are wars being fought today, but are they making our world a better place? Will there ever be an end to having to defend ourselves? I can vote for leaders who I think will negotiate peace before war but who, like you, will not hesitate to defend our country. I can pray for peace. St. Henry, pray for me.

July 14 St. Kateri Tekakwitha (1656-1680) is the first Native American to be declared blessed. When she was only four years old, smallpox took the lives of her parents and she went to live with her uncle, a Mohawk chief. Even though she knew doing so would make her an outcast with her people, she took instruction in the Catholic faith from a Jesuit missionary who visited her village and was baptized Catherine (Kateri) when she was 20 years old. Her tribe became very hostile to her and she suffered because of her faith. For her safety, she left the village and walked 200 miles to a Christian village near Montreal where she helped the missionaries and did penance to make reparation to God for the cruelty of the Indians and

European settlers toward each other. She died when she was only 24 years old. She is called the "Lily of the Mohawks" for her purity of heart.

St. Kateri Tekakwitha, you followed your heart and embraced Christianity even though it caused you to lose the support and love of your people. I take my freedom to worship as I wish for granted, but many people have to suffer, as you did, in order to worship God. How strong is my faith? Would I stay true to my beliefs even if it meant losing family and friends because of what I believe? How can I keep the name of Jesus before me at all times, especially at times when my faith is challenged? Just saying his name will make me brave enough to stand up for my beliefs. "Jesus, mercy." St. Kateri, pray for me.

July 15 St. Bonaventure (1221-1274) was elected Minister General of the Friars Minor at a time when the Franciscans were in a state of upheaval with two factions calling for completely opposite ways of following the Rule of St. Francis. One faction wanted to follow the rule closely especially its devotion to poverty while the others wanted to relax the rules. St. Bonaventure lost no time in dealing with both extremes and restored peace within the order. He wrote a biography of the life of St. Francis which was held to be the

official story of that saint's life. This humble and enthusiastic preacher was named a Doctor of the Church.

St. Bonaventure, you worked out a way to settle the difference among the Franciscans who had different but strong opinions of how the order should follow the Rule of St. Francis. You were firm but fair. I think that must be how God is. He is firm about wanting us to follow his commandments, but fair when he recognizes our weaknesses and forgives us our lapses. Am I firm but fair in my dealings with my family and friends? Do I feel superior to them when they make mistakes or do I try to help them? Do I recognize that imperfection is part of the human burden but still remain firmly committed to doing my best one day at a time? St. Bonaventure, pray for me.

July 16 Our Lady of Mount Carmel

When St. Simon Stock was praying to Our Blessed Virgin for his order, the Carmelites, that he felt was being suppressed, Our Lady appeared on this date giving him a brown scapular and promising that anyone who wore it would be saved from eternal death. It became part of the Carmelite habit. The Carmelites, founded at Mount Carmel, in Israel, in the 12th century, instituted this feast day to celebrate Our Lady's help to gain recognition for the order. The last time the Blessed Virgin appeared at Fatima, she appeared as Our Lady of Mount Carmel.

Our Lady, you are a mother to me and to everyone in the world. When we ask for your intercession with Jesus, we know you take our requests to him and ask for a loving response. I know you want what is best for my soul and I do too. When I am troubled I imagine you at my side, your love surrounding me and cushioning the blows the world deals me. I love you and I thank you for loving me. Our Blessed Mother, pray for me and all the Carmelites who have dedicated their lives to God.

July 17 St. Francis Solano (1549-1610) had such a winning personality that, while a teenager, he was able to stop a duel! He was born to a prominent Spanish family and became a Friar in 1570. After his ordination, there was a great epidemic during which he became well-known for his conscientious care for the sick. He was sent to South America where he learned the languages of the indigenous people and ministered to the sick, often playing his violin for them. He was a great defender of the poor. St. Francis believed that Christians' lives must be an example to other peoples and he lived his life according to that belief.

St. Francis Solano, you ministered not only to the physical ailments of the sick and the poor but to their spirits as well by learning their language so you could converse with them and enriching their lives with your music. God has blessed me in so many ways, but all I have really belongs to him and is given to me to be shared with others less blessed. Do I have empathy for the poor and homeless in my community? Do I share what God has given me with them? How can I model your love for the poor and be an example that others follow? With whom can I share my blessings today? St. Francis, pray for me.

July 18 St. Camillus de Lellis (1550-1614) was a big man, some say over 6 feet 6 inches, who spent his younger years as a soldier. He developed an addiction to gambling so severe that he had to take a construction job to pay his debts, working on a building for the Capuchins who converted him. He wanted to join the Capuchins, but a battle injury sent him to the hospital for the incurable instead and he ended up its administrator. When he eventually became a priest, he founded the Congregation of the Servants of the Sick. He hoped that his service to the sick might make up for his youthful sins.

St. Camillus, you were addicted to gambling, but that addiction led you to find a way to serve God. There are so many things we can become addicted to: smoking, drinking, food, drugs, sex, or gambling like you. Am I addicted to some substance or action? If I am, is there any way I can turn my addiction into a way to serve God? Can I ask for help to wean myself away from my addiction and offer the pain of withdrawal up to God? Do any members of my family or my friends have an addiction? Do I give them support and understanding? St. Camillus, pray for me.

July 19 St. Aurea (died 856) was born in Cordoba, Spain, to Muslim parents. She married, but when her husband died, she was baptized a Christian and, after taking vows to become a nun, spent the next 20 years in a convent. Her family, never reconciled to either her conversion or her choice of life, reported her to the Moorish authorities and she was beheaded.

St. Aurea, families are supposed to stand by and support each other, but your family did not give you the support and love you needed. There is a fine line between wanting to help our family members and telling them how to run their lives. Your family did not give you the freedom to live your own life. I wonder if I am guilty of that too. Do I give advice when it's not wanted? Am I hurt when my advice is not taken? Do I support my family members in their decisions and help them when they make wrong choices? St. Aurea, pray for me. I want to love and support my family in all ways.

***July 20 St. Elias or Elijah (Old Testament Prophet*)** was one of the greatest prophets of the Old Testament living in the 9th century, BC. He is often pictured as being taken up to heaven at the end of his life in a fiery chariot drawn by 4 horses and is mentioned in the holy books of many religions, not just the bible. His many recorded miracles include raising the dead, parting the waters of the sea, calling fire and rain down from the sky, and multiplying corn and oil to feed a widow. He used his miraculous powers to fight the Israelite king, Ahab, and his wicked wife, Jezebel, who worshipped the false god Baal. The gospels of Matthew, Mark, and Luke also tell of Elijah and Moses being seen with Jesus as He became transfigured and radiant on a mountaintop.

St. Elias, you were given the gift of miracles and prophecy by God and you used your powers to do good and fight against evil, especially the worshipping of false gods. There are many false gods that we worship today; wealth, fame, possessions, food, and drugs. Am I worshiping a false god? Do I value any earthly thing over God? What would my life be like if I put God first before everything and everyone else? What would it be like if I rid myself of the false gods I worship? St. Elias, pray for me.

July 21 St. Lawrence of Brindisi (1559-1619) was a brilliant scholar with great gifts for learning languages and delivering sermons. Is it any wonder then that he spent a good part of his life bringing the word of God to many nations including the Jews in Italy? His linguistic ability made it possible for him to study the bible in its original text and he used scripture as the basis of his sermons. His brilliance did not cause him to feel superior to others. Instead he had a deeply-felt compassion for the needs of those he met.

St. Lawrence, your compassion as well as your talent for delivering God's message brought many to know and serve God. Am I as compassionate as you were to those who have chosen different paths than I and whose problems seem to be self-made or am I judgmental or impatient with them? Do I remind myself that I may never understand the problems of others because I have not walked in their shoes, but I can still show them love and compassion? St. Lawrence, pray for me.

July 22 St. Mary Magdalene (1ˢᵗ century) was a sinner who repented of her sins. Once when Jesus was having supper, she came and washed his feet with her tears, anointed them with oils, and wiped them dry with her hair. Christ's host was aghast that such an evil woman would dare to go near him, but Jesus

praised her for giving him comfort as his host had not thought to do. St. Mary Magdalene was present at the crucifixion and was the first to see and be greeted by the risen Jesus.

St. Mary Magdalene, you were sorry for your sins and they were forgiven. The man who had invited Jesus to his home had not thought of giving him water to wash his feet or oil to ease them, but you thoughtfully provided those things. Am I a thoughtful person? Do I consider the feelings of others before I speak? Do I look for opportunities to help others? Do I give God my best through my love for his children? St. Mary Magdalene, pray for me.

July 23 St. Bridget (1303-1373) and her husband Ulf raised eight children before she was asked to work in the household at the court of the king of Sweden. St. Bridget was appalled at the immorality of the court and urged the king and queen to turn their lives over to God, but they ignored her pleas. She and Ulf continued to devote their lives to God and, when Ulf died, St. Bridget asked the king for money and land to build a monastery for the religious order she wanted to found. Her order of Brigittines led simple lives helping the poor and building a great library which made the monastery the intellectual center of Sweden.

St. Bridget, you and your husband did not hesitate to try

to teach the people at the king's court about God. When you were ignored, it would have been easy to slip into the immoral ways of the court, but you did not give in to that temptation. Do I sometimes go along with the crowd because it's easier? Can I avoid temptation, and if I can't, can I ignore it? Can I practice my faith no matter what others around me are doing or saying? St. Bridget, pray for me.

July 24 St. Sharbel Makhlouf (1828-1898) was a monk, born in Lebanon, who was known for his great humility and obedience. For the last 23 years of his priesthood, he lived as a hermit, offering himself as a sacrifice so that all in the world would come to worship God. When he died, all who knew him were certain that he would do great things from beyond the grave and he did. Many miracles are credited to his name.

St. Sharbel, you offered your whole life up to God so that all peoples of the world would become believers. There is so much strife in the world today, especially in the part of the world where you were born with terrorists killing innocents in God's name. Do I, in my words and actions, project the love and peace God wishes for us? Peace begins with one person. How can I be that person today and every day? St. Sharbel, pray for me.

July 25 St. James the Greater, Apostle (1st century) was mending his fishing nets with his brother John when Jesus saw them and called to them to join him. The brothers were nicknamed Sons of Thunder probably because of their fiery tempers. Jesus taught them meekness and patience. James along with Peter and John were the only witnesses to the transfiguration of Jesus when they saw Elijah and Moses by Christ's side and heard God's voice saying, "This is my Son whom I love. Listen to him." St. James was beheaded by King Herod Agrippa I, a Jewish king responsible for persecuting many Christians.

St. James, you and your brother both had hot tempers and Jesus helped you develop patience. There are times when I get angry, and do and say things I later regret. That is when I need to take a deep breath, count to ten, and pray that Jesus will help me develop that virtue just as he helped you. Can I remember to say a short prayer like, "Jesus, help me show love," when something or someone makes me angry or impatient? Wouldn't my life and the life of those around me be more peaceful if I did? St. James, pray for me.

July 26 Sts. Anne and Joachim *(1st century)* prayed for a child for many years even when it seemed useless to pray any

longer. When an angel appeared and told them that they would conceive and have a child, St. Anne promised to dedicate that child to God. That child was the Blessed Virgin Mary. We don't know a great deal about these saints, but they must have been wonderful parents to have raised a daughter who could agree to bear the child of God, who could have raised Jesus in a godly way, and who had the courage to stand by Jesus' side as he hung dying on the cross.

St. Anne and St. Joachim, you are the perfect examples of how parents should raise their children, teaching them to honor God and do his will. Do my words and actions teach love and honor for God? Am I a good example and a teacher of the faith to my family members and to all I meet? Saints Anne and Joachim, pray for me.

July 27 Sts. Natalie and Aurelius (unknown) were husband and wife. During the Moorish persecution of Christians, St. Aurelius, the son of a Moor and a Spanish woman, was secretly raised as a Christian by an aunt. He married a Moorish woman who converted to Christianity taking the name Natalie. Both of these saints were beheaded for befriending a monk and openly practicing their religion with him.

Saints Natalie and Aurelius, you were martyred for practicing your religion openly. I cannot imagine not having the freedom to worship as I want, yet there are many places in the world where people are denied that freedom. I offer this prayer for all those who are not allowed to worship God openly and freely, and I thank God that I have been given this privilege. Saints Natalie and Aurelius, pray for me and for all who are persecuted for their faith.

July 28 Blessed Anthony della Chiesa (1394-1459) led a very ordinary life except for one instance when the ship he was on was captured by pirates. His prayers swayed the pirates so much that they took all the passengers safely to shore. Born to a noble family in Italy, Blessed Anthony became a Dominican in his early twenties in spite of the objections of his family. He was a miracle worker, an excellent preacher, and a confessor who could read the conscience of men and women. He accompanied St. Bernardine on his travels and was a leader in opposing the last anti-pope. He was devoted to Our Blessed Mother and had several conversations with her while in a state of ecstasy.

Blessed Anthony, overcoming your family's objection to your religious vocation, you became an effective servant of God. You followed your conscience that was telling you to spend your life doing God's work. Do I follow my conscience all the time? I know right from wrong, but when temptation strikes, do I ignore it or do I give in to it? When have I successfully turned away from temptation? When my conscience tells me there is an opportunity to do good, do I accept the challenge? Blessed Anthony, pray for me.

July 29 St Martha (1ˢᵗ century) with her brother Lazarus and her sister Mary enjoyed a close relationship with Jesus, and He visited them at Bethany a few times. The most noted of those times was when He raised Lazarus from the dead. At that time He asked Martha if she had faith that all who believed in him would never die and her answer left no doubt as to how she felt. "Yes, Lord. I have come to believe that you are the Messiah, the Son of God, the one who is coming into the world." St. Martha focused on household work like cooking and serving food as a way to honor God.

St. Martha, you believed that anyone who loves Jesus will never die, and you spent your life serving him by serving others. You dedicated your everyday work to honor God. Can I do the same? Can I offer all my work today to him and do it in his name? St. Martha, pray for me.

July 30 St. Peter Chrysologus (406-450) has a name that is translated "Peter of the Golden Words," and is best remembered for his short, concise sermons that taught about the church as well as offered advice on how to obey God's word. Although he wrote the sermons to instruct his own parishioners, it is because of them that he was named a Doctor of the Church. St. Peter was intensely loyal to the church's authority and said that learning about the church's teachings was an obligation if we wanted to obey and love God to the best of our ability.

St. Peter, your sermons were short and to the point as you tried to educate the people you served about the church's teachings. Homilies at mass can sometimes be tediously long, and I know I don't always pay attention as I should. How can I concentrate on the message, not the speaker's talent or the length of the sermon, and come away from it with some new understanding of our church? St. Peter, pray that my ears be opened to the message of God and the Holy Spirit.

July 31 St. Ignatius Loyola (1491-1556) was a Spanish soldier in the war against the French and was wounded in battle. While he was recuperating, he read about Christ and the saints and decided to become a different kind of soldier, a

soldier of Christ. After making this decision, he went through a long period of doubts and fears, writing "The Spiritual Exercise" about this experience. When he finally earned his degree at age 43, he gathered friends to work with him for God and founded the Society of Jesus, the Jesuits.

St. Ignatius, you went through years of fearing that everything you did was sinful, worrying that you had not made sufficient confession of your sins. Some say you were almost driven to despair and thoughts of suicide. Despite this mental turmoil, you went on to work for God with much success. How much time do I spend worrying about worldly choices concerning my looks, possessions, and friends? How much time do I spend thinking about my relationship with God? Do I do my best to be a good Christian even when I am plagued by doubts? St. Ignatius, please pray that I always be aware of how my choices affect my soul.

+August Opening Prayer+

Saintly friends, as I learn about all your wonderful accomplishments here on earth, I am awed. If I can follow your lead, a path will open up before me that will guide me to the place God has reserved for me in his heavenly home. *"I will praise the Lord with my whole heart, in the assembly of the just and in the congregation. Great are the works of the Lord which must be studied by all who love them." Psalm 110:1-2*

August 1 St. Alphonsus Marie Liguori (1696-1787) was a child prodigy who became a practicing lawyer while still a teenager and was ordained a priest at age 29. He founded the Congregation of the Most Holy Redeemer in 1732. In 1777, the

government threatened to break up the order, but St. Alphonsus argued so fervently that the king reconsidered. However, the saint was tricked into agreeing to changes in the order that did not meet the approval of the church and he was removed as its leader. Despite being burdened with severe rheumatism that bent him over nearly double, a bout of rheumatic fever that left him paralyzed, and depression over being denied the right to oversee his congregation, he continued to write, prophesy, and work miracles until he died. He is a Doctor of the Church.

St. Alphonsus, you didn't let the disappointment you must have felt when you were not able to oversee the congregation you had founded, or your physical pain, stop you from serving God through your actions and your writings. Do I keep my eye on God, as you did, or am I letting physical or emotional problems keep me from doing my best in any work I do? Do I trust that, since God is with me every day, all day, I can do anything I set out to do? Do I sincerely say, "Thy will be done" and accept my daily cross? Pray for me, St. Alphonsus.

August 2 St. Eusebius of Vercelli (315-371) was a great defender of the faith against heresy. After Emperor Constantine declared Christianity the state religion, a group of Christians advanced the belief, Arianism, that Christ was not divine,

causing a schism in the church. The Pope asked St. Eusebius to attend a conference called by the emperor to settle the dispute. The Arians, unwilling to settle the differences, told everyone there that they must denounce St. Athanasius, their chief opponent. St. Eusebius would not denounce him so he was exiled during which time his enemies treated him very harshly.

St. Eusebius, you stayed loyal to a friend whose beliefs you shared just as God is always loyal to me by never withholding his love. Am I loyal to God or do I let myself be swayed by others who do not know him? How do I show my loyalty? Do I speak of God with reverence, pray to him often, and let others know how much He means to me? St. Eusebius, pray for me. I want to be a loyal servant of my Lord.

August 3 St. Lydia Purpuraria (1st century) was a businesswoman who dealt in a fine purple cloth. She, along with her entire household, was St. Paul's first convert to the church and she invited him to stay at her house. She is mentioned in Acts16:14-15. "And a certain woman named Lydia, a seller of purple from the city of Thyatria, who worshipped God, was listening and the Lord touched her heart to give heed to what was being said by Paul. And when she and her household had been baptized, she appealed to us and said,

'If you have judged me to be a believer in the Lord, come into my house and stay there.' And she insisted upon our coming."

St. Lydia, your life was changed because you listened to what Paul was saying and became a Christian. How would my life change if I really listened to the homilies preached at church services and tried to live up to what they tell me? Am I really a part of what is happening during services, or am I just an onlooker? St. Lydia, pray for me. I want to be a good listener.

August 4 Saint John Vianney (1786-1859) had little formal schooling so when he decided to become a priest he struggled with understanding the lectures which were given in Latin. Not ready to give up his dream, he worked with a tutor and, after intensive study, was ordained. This was the way this saint met all challenges, with hard work and faith that God would show the way. He founded a home for girls, worked up to 16 hours every day as a confessor, and performed works of charity, while his nights were a time of torment from the devil. Advocating public prayer, he felt that prayers from many people praying together were "like a huge bonfire rather than a lot of scattered flames."

St. John Vianney, often I set a goal and then, because the way to accomplish that goal is hard, I give up. That was not your way. You realized your dream of becoming a priest through persistence, hard work, and faith that God would help you, and you continued to meet all of life's challenges in that same way. When I meet challenges, do I remind myself that nothing is too hard for me and God to do together? Do I pray as if the outcome is all up to God and work as if the outcome is all up to me? St. John, pray for me. I want to accomplish something good for God.

August 5 Dedication of the Basilica of St. Mary Major in Rome

In the early days of the church some claimed that Mary was not the Mother of God. In 431 the Council of Ephesus resolved the issue and Pope Sixtus III then rebuilt and renamed this church which is the largest church in the world honoring God through Mary, his mother. It was the first basilica erected in honor of our Blessed Mother. There is a legend that the man who owned the land where the basilica stands had a dream that there would be snow on the land on August 5 which was preposterous as Rome swelters in the summer. Strangely enough, Pope Sixtus had the same dream. On that date, both men traveled to the plot of land and they could not believe their eyes when they did indeed see snow. The land was dedicated to the Blessed Virgin from that moment on.

Blessed Mary, Mother of God, you gave birth to Jesus, and it is right that we should always honor you as He would want us to honor his mother. Do I give you the respect and honor you deserve by praying your special prayer, the rosary? Do I honor my earthly mother and recognize that, although she is only human and not perfect, she deserves respect too? Mary, I love you and believe you love me as any mother loves her child. I pray that I may be worthy of that love and that someday I will be with you in heaven. Mary, mother of God and my mother, pray for me.

August 6 Feast of the Transfiguration of the Lord

When Jesus led Peter, James, and John up Mount Tabor, they had no idea of the vision they would see there. Before their eyes, Jesus was transfigured; his face shone like the sun and his garments appeared white as snow. Moses and Elijah appeared with him and, from a cloud that cast its shadow over them, they heard a voice say, "This is my beloved Son with whom I am well pleased; listen to him." Jesus told his apostles that the suffering He was going to endure and the glory that would come after were connected, reassuring them that our suffering here on earth will be followed by unimaginable glories in the afterlife.

Jesus, you suffered willingly for me and my sins so that someday, after my worldly life is ended, I will be able to join you in Heaven. When my path is not easy, when I am tempted, when my faith is challenged, I will remember your words and do my best to follow your example so that I may be transfigured too and share the glory that you earned for me. Jesus, I love and I trust in you.

August 7 St. Sixtus II and His Companions (d. 258) were martyrs of the early church. St. Sixtus did not shirk from accepting the responsibility of becoming the church's leader even though being pope, at that time, was like having a death sentence pronounced against you. St. Sixtus was elected pope at the same time that the emperor Valerian forbade Christians to meet together in assembly. In 258, only one year after he assumed his office, while celebrating Mass in a catacomb, he and four of his deacons were seized. When they refused to give up their faith, they were beheaded. In the days that followed at least two other deacons were killed as well as St. Lawrence, his archdeacon, four days later.

St. Sixtus, you did not hesitate to assume a responsibility that you knew would bring you pain and certain death. You stayed true to your beliefs and inspired others to do the same. I am called to affirm my faith everyday through what I say and what I do. Do my actions and words proclaim what I believe? Do they say to others that I am a Christian? Do they encourage others to follow God? St. Sixtus, pray for me.

August 8 St. Dominic (1170-1221) traveled for many years fighting the Albigensian heresy. This heresy declared that anything physical was bad, only the spiritual was good, and denied the Incarnation and the Church's sacraments. At one point, discouraged that the battle was not going well, he appealed to Our Blessed Mother who appeared to him and told him to pray the rosary and all would be well. St. Dominic and his companions prepared reasonable and thoughtful arguments to use in discussions with heretics winning them back to the teachings of the church. He founded the Order of Preachers, the Dominicans, devoted to converting people to the faith through preaching.

St. Dominic, you spent your life bringing people into the church and strengthening the faith of others who were being led away from its teachings. When someone makes a remark to me that shows they have a misconception about our faith, do I correct the false assumption? Do I share my faith with others in a clear and logical way as you did? Am I prepared through prayer and study to defend my faith? St. Dominic, pray for me. I want to lead others to God.

August 9 St. Theresa Benedicta of the Cross (1891-1942) was born Edith Stein of German Jewish parents, but by age 13 she had become an atheist. A brilliant woman who earned a doctorate in philosophy, she taught university students and was a prolific writer. Reading a book about St. Teresa of Avila, she became convinced that belonging to the Catholic Church was the way to find "Truth." In 1934, she entered the Carmelite order of nuns. St. Theresa had spoken to God telling him that she would be glad to share the cross of the Nazi's persecution of the Jews. St. Theresa was put to death in Auschwitz on August 9, 1942, carrying out her promise to share the burden of the cross.

St. Theresa Benedicta of the Cross, you searched for truth and found it, seemingly by chance, in the life of St. Teresa of Avila. Was it by chance or was this conversion in God's plan for you? What is God's plan for me? Am I listening to him and looking for ways to serve him? Do I have the courage to say yes as you did to any work He wants me to do and to any cross that comes my way? St. Teresa Benedicta of the Cross, pray for me.

August 10 St. Laurence (died c. 258) was asked by the emperor to give him all the treasures of the church. St. Laurence gathered all the poor who the church supported and lined them up before the emperor saying, "Here are our treasures." He was condemned to die by slowly burning and legend has it that, after some time in the flames, he said, "I am cooked enough on one side; you may turn me over." His love for God was so great he could ignore the pain of burning.

St. Laurence, you knew what the emperor wanted, but you presented him with the real treasures of the church. Do I consider the poor who need my help treasures or do I avoid them? How can I bring myself to feel true love for the needy, for my brothers and sisters who have not been given the blessings that I have? Is there something I can do today for someone who is needy? St. Laurence, pray for me.

August 11 St. Clare (c. 1193-1253) was born into a wealthy family in Assisi. When she was 18 years old, she met St. Francis of Assisi and decided she was called to serve God and live a religious life. Running away from home, she asked St. Francis for help. She took her religious vows and went on to found the Poor Clares leading it for 40 years. The nuns lived a life of prayer, silence, and fasting and kept the Franciscan

principles of absolute poverty and simplicity. One time, the convent was about to be raided by soldiers. St. Clare, unable to walk because of illness, asked to be carried to the wall surrounding the convent where she laid the Blessed Sacrament as she knelt and prayed for help. Suddenly something frightened the soldiers and they ran off.

St. Clare, in spite of your family's objections, you gave up a luxurious life for one of extreme sacrifice. You knew that whatever sacrifices you made here on earth would be overshadowed by the great glory of being united with God in heaven. What sacrifices can I make to show God that spending eternity with him is more important than anything here on earth? Can I give up a special food I like or do something kind for someone anonymously? Can I do one little thing today? St. Clare, pray for me.

August 12 St. Louis of Toulouse (1274-1297) was taken to the King of Aragon's court as a hostage as part of a political pact to free his father, Charles II of Naples and Sicily, who had been taken prisoner. When his older brother died, he became heir to the throne, but upon receiving his freedom, he renounced his title, became a Franciscan, and was appointed Bishop of Toulouse. As bishop, he wore the plain dress of his order and marked 75% of his income to feed the poor and keep

up churches. He observed the Franciscan vows of poverty, chastity, and obedience and said that Jesus was all he needed.

St. Louis, you could have reigned as king, but you chose to live a simple life, even as bishop, practicing poverty, chastity, and obedience. You didn't miss all the things you gave up. Jesus was all you needed. Do I practice poverty by giving generously to the poor, chastity by not watching any TV shows that promote promiscuity, obedience by obeying God's commandments? Do I make Jesus the center of my life so that He is all I need or do all my "things," my worldly possessions, mean too much to me? St. Louis, pray for me.

August 13 Sts. Pontian and Hippolytus (died 235) were sent to work in the mines at Sardinia and died there of exhaustion and ill treatment. St. Pontian was a pope who was exiled by the Roman Emperor Maximinus. He resigned his position when he was sent away so a new pope could be elected. Hippolytus was a pope too, although an antipope who had himself elected because he thought the leadership of the church was too lax. When he was exiled to Sardinia he surrendered his claim to the papacy. He and St. Pontian reconciled their differences before they both died in what was essentially a concentration camp.

Sts. Pontian and Hippolytus, before you died you both made an effort to understand each other's views and so you went to your death reconciled. In our world today there are many different views and beliefs on all subjects including God, heaven, and morals. Do I make an effort to understand the beliefs of others and, at the same time, explain my beliefs clearly? Do I reconcile differences between myself and others who believe differently so we have a peaceful relationship? Does what I say and do influence others to believe in God and follow his moral guidelines? Holy saints, pray for me.

August 14 St. Maximilian Mary Kolbe (1894-1941) was a Polish priest who had a special devotion to Our Blessed Mother. Despite battling tuberculosis, he started a movement, the Knights of Mary Immaculate, to spread devotion to Our Lady and he also organized communities called the Cities of the Immaculate. One was near Nagasaki, Japan, and was amazingly left unharmed when the atomic bomb was dropped there. Another, near Warsaw, Poland, gave refuge to 3000 Polish refugees during World War II. St. Maximilian was imprisoned in Auschwitz during that war and offered to be put to death in place of another prisoner. He and nine others were slowly starved to death until only he was left alive. The Nazis injected him with carbolic acid to end his life.

St. Maximilian, you didn't let your physical infirmities stop you from the working to spread devotion to Mary, and you didn't hesitate to offer your life so that another might live. In this, you followed in Christ's footsteps who gave his life for us. Do I give excuses for not doing good works when I am not feeling well or when I just don't feel like giving of myself? Do I expect others to make sacrifices instead of me? What can I do today to show my love for all God's children? St. Maximilian, pray for me.

August 15 Assumption of Mary

Although we do not have a biblical account of Mary being raised to Heaven, Catholics believe that she is in heaven with Jesus in both body and soul. On November 1, 1950, Pope Pius XII declared that the Assumption of Mary was a dogma of faith, confirming what was already believed by Catholics everywhere.

Blessed Virgin Mary, Mother of Jesus, and my mother too, my mind cannot even begin to understand what it will be like to see you when it is my time to leave this world and travel to God's kingdom. Just as a child imitates a loved parent, I will do my best here on earth to imitate your devotion to God and your obedience to his commands even when they cause pain and sorrow. Holy Mary, Mother of God, pray for me now and at the hour of my death. Amen

August 16 St. Stephen of Hungary (969-1038) was born a pagan but was baptized along with his father when he was ten years old. While king of the Magyars, he united them into one nation defeating other Magyar pagan nobles including his powerful uncle. The pope sent St. Stephen a crown and officially recognized him as Christian King of Hungary. St. Stephen worked to advance the church in his country by discouraging paganism and setting up dioceses, building cathedrals, and founding a monastery, an abbey, and a nunnery, all complete with schools. He wanted to retire to live a contemplative life, but when his oldest son died, he had no one to succeed him.

St. Stephen, you succeeded in uniting the people under your rule and you did everything you could to build a Christian nation. After working so hard you wanted to retire and spend your days meditating, but that was not the path God meant you to take, so you continued to do his work. Do I accept disappointment graciously, as you did, when I don't get something I've prayed for or do I let setbacks sour my life? Do I trust that God answers my prayers in a way that is best for my soul and look for the good in whatever happens? St. Stephen, pray for me.

August 17 St. Joan of the Cross (1666-1736) was intent on acquiring wealth as the owner of a shop inherited from her parents

in Anjou, France. She had no sympathy or compassion for the poor people she encountered and was known to be a greedy woman. Then she met an old beggar woman who claimed to be close to God. Somehow the woman changed St. Joan's attitude so that she began devoting her life to helping the poor even closing her shop so she could have more time for her charity work. She founded the Congregation of St. Anne of Providence and established religious houses, hospices, and schools.

We see from your life story, St. Joan, that others have an enormous ability to influence us. The beggar woman you met brought you closer to God, but sometimes those we meet can lead us away from God. Who among my friends or acquaintances is leading me down roads that are repugnant to God and who are encouraging me to live a life that will lead me to his kingdom? Who am I influencing and in what way? Pray for me, St. Joan of the Cross. Help me avoid those who would lead me away from God and help me influence others to seek and find him.

August 18 St. Jane Frances de Chantal (1562-1641) lived through much sadness including times of spiritual dryness and questions about her faith, but she remained a cheerful person and, inspired by Saint Francis De Sales, founded the

Order of the Visitation for widows. While she was married, she bore seven children, three of whom died in infancy. When her husband died, her disagreeable father-in-law insisted that she live with him or he would disinherit her children. Later her son was killed in battle, both her daughter-in-law and son-in-law died, and she had to resolve problems within the community she had founded along with criticism from church authorities.

St. Jane, you lost your husband when you were very young with four children to raise. It is hard to lose anyone you love, but more so when it is someone you rely on for support, emotionally and financially. Your trust in God helped you through that hard time. When loved ones die, we feel inconsolable and we question God as to why that person was taken from us. Some may even turn away from him in anger. How can I develop that same trust you had so that, when I am faced with grief, I can turn to God and be comforted? St. Jane, pray for me.

August 19 St. John Eudes (1601-1680) volunteered to care for people who were infected with the dreaded plague and, so he wouldn't infect those in his religious community, lived in a large cask in the middle of a field while doing so. This concern for others was evident throughout his entire life. He was born in Normandy, France, the son of a farmer. Ordained a

priest in 1625, he was driven by a concern for the needs of his fellow man and his great love for the Sacred Heart of Jesus and the Immaculate Heart of Mary. He founded the Sisters of Charity of the Refuge to help poor prostitutes and a religious community called the Eudists. He established seminaries so that the clergy would have a place to grow spiritually and he preached many missions to churchgoers to heighten their faith and bring them closer to God.

St. John Eudes, you were concerned for all people no matter what their station in life. You looked beyond their outward appearance and saw their inner souls. When I meet someone who is different from me, do I too look beyond what I see? Do I recognize and treat all people as my brothers and sisters in God? Do I offer help where help is needed? St. John Eudes, pray for me.

August 20 St. Bernard of Clairvaux (1091-1153) was famous for his ability to successfully arbitrate disputes, and he was called upon to settle many, including a schism involving an antipope. When St. Bernard was 22, he and almost forty of his relatives and friends joined a monastic community, reviving it so that, within four years, it had grown enough to build a new house and name Bernard as abbot. The Pope urged St. Bernard

to preach about the Second Crusade throughout Europe and, despite the fact that he did not approve, he obeyed, and his sermons helped to assemble a huge army. St. Bernard had a great affection for the Blessed Mother; his sermons and writings about her are well-known.

St. Bernard, you were able to resolve many disputes through counseling and arbitration. Situations come up in my life where I need your listening skills, your sense of fairness, and your persuasive powers to encourage resolution. Do I listen carefully when there are disagreements? Am I fair in my judgments? Do I try to bring people together so that problems can be solved peacefully? St. Bernard, pray for me.

August 21 St. Pius X (1835-1914) was born into a poor family and he never forgot his humble beginnings. In fact he felt that the pomp of the papacy, including the elaborate clothes he had to wear, was embarrassing. St. Pius encouraged people to become active politically and acted courageously in refusing to grant the French government control over affairs of the Church even when France threatened to confiscate church property. Two weeks after World War I began, St. Pius died saying, "I would gladly give my life to save my poor children from this ghastly scourge."

St. Pius X, you encouraged people to become politically active so that they might have a say in how they are governed. How active am I in exercising my right to participate in my government? Do I vote? Do I read about and understand the issues? Do I volunteer my work for good causes and the politicians who advance them? St. Pius X, pray for me.

August 22 Queenship of Mary is a feast day established by Pope Pius XII in 1954 celebrating the Blessed Virgin Mary as Queen of Heaven. He stated that she deserves to be called Queen because as the Mother of God she is closely aligned with her son, our king, and because she has great power in interceding with Jesus for us. We recognize her Queenship in many of the hymns we sing today in our churches as we hail our holy Queen.

Mary, Queen of Heaven, your role as mother of God earned you your heavenly crown. As Catholics, we believe that you were taken, body and soul, into heaven and crowned Queen. I know that you listen to my prayers and ask Jesus to reply to them. I want so much to see you someday. The most important thing I can do is live my life as you lived yours with perfect acceptance of God's will. Mary, Queen of Heaven, help me follow your example.

August 23 St. Rose of Lima, Peru (1586-1617) is a shining example of how we should concern ourselves more with spiritual matters than with physical ones, especially in today's world where appearance seems to be so important. St. Rose was very beautiful but didn't want her beauty to lead her into sin so she cut her hair, wore shabby clothes, and rubbed her face with pepper so it was disfigured. To help support the family, she gardened and made needlework. St. Rose refused to marry and joined the Third Order of St. Dominic living for many years in a small hut praying, fasting, and caring for the sick. When she died, the entire city came to pay homage and important dignitaries took turns carrying her casket. She is the first canonized saint of the New World.

St. Rose, you put no value on your great beauty but saw it as a path away from God. Am I more concerned with my outer appearance than with the state of my soul? Do I take more time with my clothes and hair than I do praying? Do I put God and my faith first in my life realizing that things of this world are fleeting and only God is eternal? St. Rose, pray for me.

August 24 St. Bartholomew, Apostle (1st century) is believed by scholars to be one and the same with the apostle Nathaniel. Not much is known about St. Bartholomew, but

whatever name you give this saint, we do know that he traveled extensively to Mesopotamia, Persia, Egypt, Armenia, and other countries to share the gospel of Christ. He was very successful in converting many to the faith, but his missionary work ended when he was flayed alive and beheaded by order of the King of Armenia.

St. Bartholomew, you were privileged to be one of Christ's apostles. You spent your life preaching to others about him so they might know the faith you loved so much you gave your life for it. Do I share my beliefs with others in the hopes that one day they will know the love and joy found only in Jesus? Do I let my actions speak of the love I feel for him? St. Bartholomew, pray for me. I want to share my love of God with others.

August 25 St. Louis of France (1226-1270) was a peacemaker and an advocate for justice. Under his rule, the nation was at peace for many years. He initiated a system of trial through witness examination and the use of written records in courts. During one of the two crusades that he led to the Holy Land, his army was captured, but he negotiated its liberation by paying a ransom in addition to surrendering the city of Damietta for his own release. He was concerned not just

for his soldiers but for all his subjects and built cathedrals, orphanages, libraries and hospitals for them. He and his wife Marguerite had ten children whose descendants ruled France until Louis XVI was led to the guillotine in 1793.

St. Louis, you ruled your people with justice and compassion, and you brought peace to a land that had been under turmoil for many years. You always treated people, even the most humble, as you hoped God would treat you. Do I always "do unto others as I would have them do unto me"? Do I forgive faults in myself that I do not forgive in others? Am I selfish or giving of my time and my money? St. Louis, pray for me.

August 26 St. Joseph Calasanz (1556-1648) couldn't persuade existing schools to educate poor children. So he and some friends started a free school in Rome, but soon saw that the need was greater than they'd thought and, with the support of the Pope, opened more schools. The teachers organized into a community, the Clerks Regular of Religious Schools, with St. Joseph as its superior. Because many influential people at that time did not believe in educating the poor, the community was suppressed after investigations by papal commissions. St. Joseph believed that in time others would see the importance

of his mission and he forgave those who had caused the turmoil. The community was recognized after St. Joseph's death.

St. Joseph Calasanz, you started a worthy movement, only to see it shattered by misunderstandings and political maneuverings. You forgave those who had caused you harm, and you waited patiently for the day when the community you founded would be recognized once again. How much patience do I have with others and with waiting for something I want? Am I forgiving of others when they hurt me in some way or when they stand in the way of my goals? St. Joseph Calasanz, pray for me. I want to be patient and forgiving too.

August 27 St. Monica (322-387) married a pagan, a man named Patricius who was not the best of husbands. They had three children; the oldest and most famous one was St. Augustine. St. Monica prayed for her husband to accept the faith of Jesus and, after many years, one year before his death, Patricius became a Christian. Augustine, however, refused over and over to be baptized claiming that the beliefs of Christians were wrong. Monica prayed and fasted for years hoping for Augustine's conversion. Soon after Augustine at long last was baptized, St Monica, having completed what she saw as her

work on earth, died. Troubled parents often turn to her for help.

St. Monica, you fasted and prayed for your husband and for St. Augustine for years, and your persistence and patience produced results. You are an inspiration to anyone who has family members who have turned their backs on God. How long do I have to pray to bring someone back to the church? Only God knows that. My job is to do what you did and not lose hope that someday my prayers will be answered. St. Monica, pray for me.

August 28 St. Augustine (354-430) never did anything by halves! He immersed himself passionately in a sinful, hedonistic lifestyle and then just as ardently embraced a Christian life focused on avoiding the sins of the flesh. He recorded the meaning of his life before and after his conversion to Christianity in the famous "Confessions." It was very difficult for Augustine to give up his life of worldly pleasures and, even after he had recognized the truth of Christianity, he chose not to be baptized. Finally he found inspiration in the scriptures, was baptized, became a priest, then bishop of Hippo in North Africa. His vast collection of writings has influenced every part of Christian doctrine.

St. Augustine, it took you a long time to realize that

worldly pleasures cannot bring true happiness. It is hard to give up habits or activities that are pleasurable, but lead us away from God. Is there anything I am doing now that is not good for my soul? If there is, what can I substitute in its place? If I read scripture, will I be inspired, as you were, to become a better person? St. Augustine, pray for me.

August 29 Beheading of St. John the Baptist (1ˢᵗ century). This saint was not afraid to remind people of how they should live their lives. When Herod, Tetrach of Galilee, began living with his niece, Herodias, who was also the wife of his half-brother Philip, St. John criticized him. Angry, Herod threw him into prison. Herodias wanted to destroy John and found her chance to do so after her daughter Salome danced for the king. King Herod had promised Salome anything she wanted. Herodias told her to ask for St. John's head on a platter which is the gift he gave her. When they heard of the beheading, St. John's disciples laid his body in a tomb.

St. John the Baptist, you helped many people along the road to Jesus by washing away their sins in the river's waters. You were not afraid to speak out against the immoral actions of Herod. Do I speak up when I see a friend or family member tempted to do something immoral? Instead of condemning them, do I try to help them choose a better path? Am I myself guilty of any immoral actions? St. John the Baptist, pray for me. I want to be an example and a gentle reminder to those around me of the way Jesus wants us to live.

August 30 St. Jeanne Jugan (1792-1879) was raised as a Catholic in France at the time of the French Revolution. She worked as a domestic, a hospital worker caring for the poor and sick, and a spinner, giving the money she made to the poor along with most of her possessions. She begged for money to help the poor, especially poor widows and, as others began working with her in her mission, founded the Little Sisters of the Poor. Blessed Jeanne served as superior of the group until she was unfairly removed from that position. She did not complain about the injustice, but continued to do her best to help the poor. It wasn't until after she died that she was recognized as the foundress of the order.

St. Jeanne Jugan, you dedicated your whole life to helping those who had nothing and you influenced others to do the same. You deserved earthly recognition, but that didn't come until after your death. Do I understand that, while it is human to want to be recognized for the work we do, the true reward will come in Heaven? Can I remember not to brag or look for praise from others and not to complain when I don't get it? St. Jeanne Jugan, pray for me that whatever good I do, I do for love of God, not praise on earth.

August 31 Sts. Joseph of Arimathea and Nicodemus (1st century) were a part of the life of Jesus. St. Joseph of Arimathea was a prominent Jewish leader who had the courage to ask for the body of Jesus when it was taken down from the cross. Wrapping the body in fine linens, he brought it to the tomb. It is possible that St. Joseph was punished for this act of love. Nicodemus was another important Jewish leader who sought Jesus in secret to learn more about his teaching. He defended Jesus at his arrest and helped with the burial.

Sts. Joseph and Nicodemus, it took a lot of courage to defend Jesus and then take his body for burial. Your love for our Savior overcame any fear you must have felt. Because God is always at our side, we never need to fear anything in this life. How can I convince myself of that? I know it is true just as I know God's love will carry me through any troubles I face, but it is so easy to forget that when I am afraid. Holy saints, pray for me. Help me think of your courage when I am facing my fears.

+September Opening Prayer+

How do I follow in your footsteps, holy saints? How do I do good here on earth and bring glory to God? How do I show love to my neighbors? *"Good works are the links that form the chain of love." Mother Teresa*

September 1 St. Giles (8th century) is mostly known through legends. He was a hermit, probably a monk, who lived in the eighth century and shunned prosperity and fame. In fact he left Athens for Marseilles to avoid honors from his countrymen and established a hermitage at the mouth of the Rhone River. Legend tells us that he lived on herbs, wild roots, and the milk of a deer he had befriended. One day, hunters came after the deer and accidentally shot St. Giles in the knee with an arrow. He refused to have the wound cared for and remained crippled for the rest of his life and, because of this,

220

has become known as a patron saint for the handicapped. He is often depicted as an old man with an arrow in his knee holding a deer. St. Giles was admired throughout Western Europe; his relics are laid to rest in a monastery named after him; and many churches bear his name.

St. Giles, your fame spread even though you lived your life quietly, avoiding praise. You cared for all creatures of the world and lived a simple life depending on God's goodness to provide. Do I have the same trust? Do I believe that, as God cares for the birds and the lilies of the field, he will care for me? St. Giles, pray for me, that my trust in God might be strong.

September 2 Blessed John Francis Burte` and Companions (d. 1792)

The French Revolution was a terror-filled time for many including a group of almost 200 priests and bishops who refused to take an oath that would in effect say that the state had supremacy over the Church. They were held in a Carmelite church waiting to be deported as enemies of the Revolution when a mob of French citizens broke into the church. The clergy were asked again if they would swear to the supremacy of the state, and, to a man, they refused. The mob then took the prisoners, two by two, and slaughtered them.

Blessed John Francis Burte`, you and your companions faced a brutal death at the hands of a mob, yet you held firm to your beliefs. This kind of courage comes from faith that God will always take care of his people. Do I have the courage to stand up for my beliefs no matter what the consequences, whether it's loss of a friendship, worldly goods, or even my life? Do I believe with all my heart that God will always take care of me because He loves me? Blessed John Francis Burte` and companions, pray for me. I want to be a courageous follower of Jesus.

September 3 St. Gregory the Great (540-604) said that, while it was hard to give up one's possessions, it is harder still to give up a person's individuality. This saint did both. First, he used his wealth and possessions to establish several monasteries. Then he gave up his quiet life as a monk to succeed Pope Pelagius II and earned the name "Gregory the Great" by his strong leadership. St. Gregory persuaded the Lombards, an aggressive people who were leading raids throughout Italy, to withdraw and leave Rome in peace; he reformed the liturgy and church music; he sent monks to spread the gospel in England; and he encouraged the growth of monasticism. He is one of the four most important Doctors of the Church.

St. Gregory, you were content to live your life as a lowly monk, and the years you spent at your monastery are said to be among the happiest of your life. Yet, when you were called to serve, you did so willingly. We all are called to serve God in some way. How will God call me to serve him? Will I recognize his call and accept it as you did? Am I willing to sacrifice my time to do what He asks of me? St. Gregory, pray for me that I might be an enthusiastic servant of God.

September 4 St. Rose of Viterbo (1235-1252) had a vision of the Blessed Mother when she was only eight years old and became a Franciscan nun at Our Lady's request. At that time, Viterbo, Italy, was dominated by Emperor Frederick, an enemy of the Church. St. Rose went through the streets preaching and urging her fellow citizens to rebel against the emperor's army. For two years St. Rose continued her preaching until she and her family were sent into exile where she continued to share God's word. After Frederick died, Rose and her family returned to Viterbo. She died at age 17. Her incorrupt body lies at the convent of St. Mary of the Roses, a convent she had dreamed of entering when she was younger.

St. Rose of Viterbo, because of your holiness, you were privileged to see the Blessed Virgin Mary in a vision. You were so young and yet you were not afraid to denounce the enemies of the Church. Do I have the courage to speak out when someone makes a belittling or derogatory remark about my faith? Do I know enough about the church's teachings to correct a mistaken idea about the church? When will I take the time to learn about some part of church doctrine that is unclear to me? St. Rose, pray for me.

September 5 Blessed Mother Teresa of Calcutta (1910-1997) felt called to enter the Sisters of Loretto to do missionary work in India. She taught school there until she contracted tuberculosis and received a second call, this one to leave the order and tend to the poor. Receiving permission to leave her order, she started a school in the slums of Calcutta and studied basic medicine so she could treat the sick. In1949, joined by some of her former students, she gathered up people who were left to die in the streets and gave them care and shelter until their death. Mother Teresa's group, which grew to thousands located in almost 500 centers all over the world, was recognized by the church as the Missionaries of Charity.

Blessed Mother Teresa, you were only one small person, but you started a movement that continues to help the poor all over the world. Recognized as a peacemaker by the world, you cared for awards only if they could further your work with the poor. Do I live by your words, "works of love are works of peace," and do my best to bring love and peace to those around me? Do I recognize those who need help and do what I can for them with love and understanding? Blessed Mother Teresa, pray for me as I try to act with love today.

September 6 Blessed Bertrand of Garrigue (c.1195-1230) was a good friend and companion to St. Dominic helping him found the order of Friar Preachers and working with him to fight a French heresy. He was a Cistercian priest, extremely holy with so many miracles attributed to him that some thought of him as the second Dominic. Blessed Bertrand, however, in his humility, witnessed instead to Dominic's life and sanctity and disavowed any attempt to compare his life to Dominic's.

Blessed Bertrand, you were a humble man for, rather than have the light of recognition shine on your work and the miracles you performed, you focused attention on St. Dominic, your friend. Friendship is a gift. Am I a good friend? Am I genuinely happy when my friends succeed or am I envious? Do I share my friends' burdens as well as their joys? Do I extend my hand in friendship to anyone who may have need of a friend? Do I keep close to the greatest friend I will ever have,

Jesus? Blessed Bertrand, pray for me; I want to be a good friend.

September 7 Blessed Frederick Ozanam (1813-1853) organized a discussion club where Catholics debated issues with atheists and agnostics. One day, a club member asked Blessed Frederick if he did anything to show his faith besides speak about it. This question made Frederick rethink his life. He soon began offering help to those living in the Paris tenements and, with the backing of St. Vincent De Paul, others joined him in his good works. After the Revolution of 1848, many French were out of work and hungry. Frederick and the Vincentians, at the request of the government, helped get aid to the poor. Frederick also started a newspaper, the *New Era*, to seek justice for the poor.

Blessed Frederick, you were concerned for those who had little and you put your words into action. It is easy to talk about what should be done to conquer poverty and injustice, but the test of our concern lies in our actions. Are words all I offer the poor, the sick, the lonely, and the oppressed? How can I put my words into action and offer help to my brothers and sisters under God? Blessed Frederick, pray for me that my words lead to actions that effect a change for good.

September 8 Birth of Our Blessed Mother Mary

Not much is said in the gospels about the birth of Mary. We know that she was born to Saints Anne and Joachim who promised they would dedicate their long-awaited child to God. We know that her birth must have been a source of wonder and delight to her parents for they had prayed for a long time for a child. We also know that God marked Mary from her birth as the future mother of his earthly Son, and so this day calls for great celebration, the day when the Mother of Jesus and the Mother of us all was born.

Mary, my Mother, when you came into this world, you were already destined for one of the greatest tasks God would ever ask of anyone. God honored you with his Son and you honor us with your love for us. Do I honor you, Mary, by imitating your holiness and praying your rosary? Do I follow your example of accepting, without protest, the Father's will no matter where it leads me? Our Blessed Virgin, pray for me.

September 9 St. Peter Claver (1581-1654) was a Jesuit priest who worked in the service of African slaves in Colombia, South America, which was the biggest slave market in the New World. He climbed on ships as they docked, gave the slaves food and water, and cared for the sick and dying. Teaching the

slaves about Jesus was an important part of his mission, and he baptized more than 300,000 slaves in his lifetime. In addition, he fought to abolish the slave trade and visited slaves on plantations encouraging owners to treat them kindly.

St. Peter Claver, you were kindness itself to those deprived of their dignity. You really were God's hands on earth. There are many people today whose dignity has been stripped from them: the homeless, prisoners, the mentally ill, and the old and abandoned. Do I treat everyone with dignity? Do I speak out when I see someone being treated disrespectfully? Is there any way I can help someone regain the dignity that God intends for every human being? Pray for me, St. Peter Claver. I want to serve Jesus by serving others.

September 10 St. Thomas of Villanova (1488-1555) went about naked many times as a child because he insisted on giving his clothes to the poor. This extraordinary charity continued his entire life. It is said that he even sold his straw mattress and mended his clothing himself, preferring to use his money to help the poor, feeding hundreds every day at his table. Determined to end the cycle of the poor relying on charity, he found work for them or bought them tools and supplies so they themselves could find work. Today the

Augustinians celebrate his life and that of Nicholas of Tolentine, two priests of the order who have been canonized.

St Thomas, you kept the poor before you always, sacrificing your own comfort for their benefit. There are so many people in the world today who have no place to call their own and not enough food to eat. God had given me so much and I know He wants me to share. How can I do the most good? Can I donate money and goods to charities that help the homeless? Can I volunteer at a homeless shelter, help distribute food, or work with organizations that build homes for the homeless? St. Thomas, help me find ways to share my blessings. Pray for me and for all the poor.

September 11 St. Cyprian (c. 200-258) was the Bishop of Carthage during the persecutions of the Roman emperor Decius. Rather than face death, many Christians substituted pagan practices for their religious rites while others signed certificates saying they had sacrificed to pagan gods. When the persecutions ended, these former Christians wanted to return to the Church. St. Cyprian was among those who felt that those who had not actually worshipped idols should be readmitted under strict conditions, if they felt true remorse, while those who had worshipped idols could receive communion on their deathbed.

St. Cyprian, you treated the fallen away Christians just as God would have done; God forgives us all things if we repent. Because I am human, I know that sometimes what I do is not pleasing to God. Do I always recognize when I have sinned? Do I take the time to tell Jesus that I am sorry and will try not to commit that sin again? If someone sins against me, do I forgive them and give them another chance just as God does? St. Cyprian, pray for me.

September 12 Blessed Maria Victoria Fornari (1562-1617) was in a state of despair after her husband died leaving her with five children and a sixth on the way. She prostrated herself in front of a statue of the Blessed Virgin and heard the Virgin telling her not to worry because she would take care of her. After that, Blessed Maria picked up the pieces of her life and cared for the sick, helped young girls who had strayed, and worked with slaves to prepare them for baptism. After all of her children had entered the religious life, she started a community of nuns called the Celestial Annunciades. Today we also celebrate the feast day of the Holy Name of Mary.

Blessed Maria Victoria Fornari, you were ready to give up in despair when Our Blessed Virgin raised you out of the darkness. I believe she stands ready to help all her children when they can't see light at the end of their path. Do I really think of Mary as my mother? Is the holy name of Mary in my prayers when I feel like I can't go on? Can I picture her holding my hand throughout all my troubles and feel her great love? Holy Mother and Blessed Maria, pray for me.

September 13 St. John Chrysostom (c. 347-407) was a very skilled orator; his name means "Golden Mouth." During his tenure as Archbishop of Constantinople, he was falsely accused of several crimes against the Emperor and was banished twice. He bore all injustice with dignity and in a famous quote said, "Violent storms encompass me on all sides; yet I am without fear, because I stand upon a rock. Though the seas roar and the waves rise high, they cannot overwhelm the ship of Jesus Christ. I fear not death, which is my gain; nor banishment, for the whole earth is the Lord's; nor the loss of goods, for I came naked into the world, and I can carry nothing out of it."

St. John Chrysostom, your faith and trust in God carried you through false accusations and banishment from your country. Your words make so much sense. Wherever we go, God is there; no one can take him away from us except ourselves with our sins. He is our rock. Even though I don't know what lies ahead for me in this life, have I put my trust in God's faithfulness? Do I believe that He will be at my side through all the ups and downs? Do I go to him first with my problems instead of trying to solve them all by myself? St. John, pray for me.

September 14 Feast of the Holy Cross

In the days when the Romans were persecuting the first Christians, the cross was not a symbol of holiness. It was a symbol of death; too many lined the roads bearing the decaying bodies of dead Christians hung there for their belief in the one true God. When St. Helen, the mother of the Emperor Constantine, went to Jerusalem, she had the Temple of Aphrodite destroyed and on that site built the Basilica of the Holy Sepulcher. Legend says that, when the site was excavated, three crosses were found. The cross that bore Jesus was identified when a woman was cured of her illness after touching it.

Dear Jesus, you suffered and died for me on a wooden cross, and it is right that we venerate the cross today. The crosses I bear are not made of wood, but of worries and anxieties for myself and the ones I love. Can I offer them up to you, as you offered your suffering, for the good of the world and my loved ones? Can I carry my burdens with willingness and trust that you walk alongside of me wherever I go? Jesus, I love you and thank you for your gift to me of yourself.

September 15 St. Catherine of Genoa (1447-1510)
wanted to enter the religious life, but her parents arranged for her to marry the son of a rival family, a man who was the exact opposite of everything Catherine believed in. For ten years she struggled, first with a deep depression, then with an attempt to join with her husband in a hectic social life. One day, she was suddenly filled with a realization that she was a sinner and, as bitterness left her, she resolved to live a life of goodness doing hospital work. When her husband lost his fortune, they lived in a cottage where, following Catherine's lead, her husband gave up his immoral ways and began to lead a Christian life.

St. Catherine, you tried for many years to repress the part of you that wanted to serve God and this repression led to a bitter, unhappy life. Yet, you struggled out of depression and became a savior to the many sick that you tended and an example of what is possible when we turn to God. Do I let depression about worldly things lead me away from God? Could I overcome sadness and depression by focusing on others instead of dwelling on my own troubles? God loves me and wants me to be happy, not depressed and sad. St. Catherine, pray for me.

September 16 St. Cornelius (died 253) was chosen as pope by the governing college of priests after the church had been without a pope for over a year. His tenure lasted only two years and it was marked by great dissension. At the center of controversy was the sacrament of Penance and how those who had left the church during a time of persecution could be readmitted. Some said they should not be allowed to rejoin the church. St. Cornelius convened a synod at Rome in 251 and decreed that those who had left the church could be readmitted if they repented and did penance.

St. Cornelius, you are one of the church leaders who helped define how reconciliation with the church could be accomplished. You led the way for practices in our modern day church by imitating God's forgiveness and mercy for sinners. The sacrament of Penance not only releases me from my sins but also gives me strength to avoid temptation. Am I receiving the sacrament of Penance on a regular basis? Do I examine my conscience before I receive the sacrament? Am I really sorry for my sins and resolve never to commit them again? St. Cornelius, pray for me.

September 17 St. Robert Bellarmine (1542-1621) devoted his life to studying and writing about scripture and

Catholic doctrine. He was a rather controversial person, advocating democracy to the dismay of the kings of that era. He believed that authority comes from God and is given to the people who choose leaders to administer it. This is basically the tenets of democracy as we know it today. He protested actions of the church against Galileo with whom he had corresponded, and he was involved in disputes between kings and the church concerning papal authority. This Jesuit was also kind and self-sacrificing, giving even the drapes from his window to the poor.

St. Robert Bellarmine, you were a very talented scholar as well as a kind man and you were not afraid to stand up for what you believed even if it upset some very powerful people. Am I like you? Do I have the courage of my convictions? When I see discrimination, or abuse, or anything that goes against God's law, do I say something or take action? Do I let my elected officials know what I think? St. Robert, pray for me. I want to be an active Christian.

September 18 St. Joseph Cupertino (1603-1663), an Italian saint, knew sorrow and rejection his entire life. It was hard for him to learn, he was clumsy, and he was subject to what he called "fits of giddiness" when he went into a daze and

forgot whatever he was doing. When his family threw him out, he performed menial labor for the Franciscan Friars' saying he didn't deserve anything better in life, but soon people realized that behind the quiet exterior was a humble and unselfish person who was cheerful no matter what his circumstances. He was able to levitate, formed close ties with animals, and performed many miracles. He became a priest but members of his order were suspicious of him and he was kept in isolation for many years until he died.

St. Joseph Cupertino, you never complained about all the disappointments you met in life, but made the best of what you had, staying cheerful throughout. It is so easy to complain when things don't go my way, when I feel rejected, and when I want more than I have. Am I a complainer or, like you, do I do the best I can with what God has given me? Do I meet disappointment with cheerfulness, knowing that it is part of God's plan for me? St. Joseph, pray for me.

September 19 St. Januarius (d. 305) was only 30 years old when he was beheaded for admitting to being a Christian. Later, when the Emperor Constantine gave religious freedom to the Church, this saint's head and body along with two sealed vials of his blood were taken to Naples where they were placed in an

underground room that now lies under the present-day cathedral. Several times a year the blood in the vials passes from a solid to a liquid state, a phenomenon scientists have been unable to explain. Neapolitans credit St. Januarius with saving them from plague and from destruction from volcanic eruptions.

St. Januarius, your blood changing each year from a solid to a liquid presents us with a mystery. There are so many supernatural mysteries to think about. Where is heaven? What is it like? How can there be three persons in one in the Holy Trinity? What will God ask me on judgment day? Someday, when we are with God, we will know the answers to all our questions. Is the life I'm leading one that I am not ashamed to offer God on that last day? What can I do, right now, that will please him? St. Januarius, pray for me.

September 20 Sts. Andrew Kim Taegon, Paul Chong Hasang, and Companions (1821-1846) The Church in Korea began as a home church led by lay people who had studied Jesuit literature from China. In fact for a dozen years after the church was started, it survived without its members ever seeing a priest. St. Andrew Kim Taegon was the first Korean priest and was tortured and beheaded. Paul Chong Hasang was a lay man who was also martyred. Pope John Paul II canonized these

two men along with ninety-eight Koreans and three French missionaries, all martyred between 1839 and 1867.

St. Andrew Kim Taegon and St. Paul Chong Hasang, you and your companions suffered greatly in order for you to be able to worship God according to your beliefs. Your courage is awesome. I am so lucky to live in a land where I can worship God without fear of torture or death. What do I do to make sure my liberties are not taken away? Do I vote for officials who will safeguard these liberties for everyone? Do I pray for anyone living in lands where they cannot worship freely? Holy saints, pray for me.

September 21 St. Matthew, Apostle (I^{st} century) was a tax collector and, as such, was despised and considered a sinner by his fellow Jews. When Jesus asked him to come with him, he followed without question, leaving his former life behind to become one of the twelve Apostles. When Christ was asked why He would choose a sinner to walk with him, He answered that He had not come only to call the just, but sinners as well. St. Matthew preached Christ's way for 15 years among the Jews and wrote one of the four New Testament Gospels to try to convince them that Jesus was their Messiah.

St. Matthew, because many Jews did not recognize Jesus

as the long awaited savior, you preached to them and wrote your gospel hoping to lead them to see the truth. How many people today do not recognize that Jesus came to earth and died for our sins so that one day we might be with him in heaven? Am I doing anything to help non-believers get to know Jesus? Do my words and actions imitate his love for them? St. Matthew, pray for me.

September 22 St. Maurice and Martyrs of the Theban Legion (c. 287) were members of a Roman legion that was made up completely of Christians. When the armies paused to rest, on the brink of a battle, all soldiers were told to offer a sacrifice to the gods. St. Maurice, answering for his men, refused to pay homage to false gods. The commander ordered that the Christian Legion be decimated; one out of every ten men in the legion was executed and they were told again to offer sacrifice. Again they refused. Eventually, the entire legion was executed.

St. Maurice, you and your men showed your love for God by refusing to worship false gods. There are many false gods that surround me in today's world and it is hard not to pay homage to them. Money and things that money can buy, entertainment that leads to sin, companions who encourage

239

moral laxity: these are all false gods that tempt me into worship of them. What false gods may be tempting me right now? Do I have the courage to walk away from them and remain true to the one God I love above all else? St. Maurice, pray for me.

September 23 St. Padre Pio de Piatrelcina (1887-1968) saw Jesus before him with his hands, feet, and side dripping blood. It was September 20, 1918 and Padre Pio had just finished saying mass. After the vision disappeared, St. Padre Pio saw that he too was bleeding and for over 50 years he suffered the pain of the stigmata, but, at his death at age 81, the wounds healed without leaving scars. This saint performed thousands of miracles, had many visions of Jesus, Mary, and the saints, and was said to be able to be in two places at one time. He was a Capuchin Franciscan priest who heard confessions for ten or twelve hours every day and was actually able to see what was in penitents' hearts.

St. Padre Pio, you suffered for many years bearing the stigmata of Jesus. You are one of the few chosen ones who know firsthand the pain Jesus bore so that someday we might join him in Heaven. How can I show Jesus that I am grateful for his gift to me? Can I spend a few minutes each day thinking about his wounds and how painful they must have been? When I have pain, can I compare it to the pain of Jesus and offer it to him in thanks? What pain or disappointment am I suffering right now that I can offer up in thanksgiving? St. Padre Pio, pray for me.

September 24 St. Pacifico of San Severino (1653-1721) is best remembered for his poverty and obedience. This saint ate only enough to sustain him, mostly bread, water, and soup, and he wore a hair shirt made of iron. He was a teacher of philosophy for a time as well as a preacher of missions. When St. Pacifico was only 35 years old, he became ill and was left deaf, blind, and crippled, no longer able to preach. St. Pacifico was not a complainer. Instead of cursing his condition, he accepted the infirmities and offered his suffering so that sinners might be converted. He cured many of the sick who came to him for help.

St. Pacifico, you suffered deafness, blindness, and ill health, but you didn't complain. Instead you offered your sufferings up to God for the good of others. Sometimes it seems more satisfying to complain and receive sympathy than to suffer in silence. Can I try to imitate you the next time I'm suffering? Like you, can I accept disappointments or disabilities in silence without complaint and offer them up to God so that some good might come of them? "God is our refuge and our strength; he has proved himself greatly a helper in distress." (Psalm 46:2) St. Pacifico, pray for me.

September 25 St. Elzear (1286-1323) and Blessed Delphina (1283-1358) both had very religious upbringings and they felt bound to honor the marriage arrangement their parents had made for them. When they married in their mid-teens, they vowed perpetual virginity, joined the secular Franciscans, and devoted their lives to doing good works like caring for the poor. In fact, each night they shared their dinner table with twelve poor people. When St. Elzear became a count after his father's death, his subjects took advantage of his gentle nature, but he brought them around by treating them with love. After St. Elzear died, Blessed Delphina continued to help the poor for over 35 years.

St. Elzear and Blessed Delphina, you devoted your lives to doing good works and you treated everyone with kindness and respect. You saw God in everyone. Do I always remember that God made us all and he loves every one of us and wants us all to be united with him in Heaven? Do I treat everyone with respect? Do I judge people by what is in their hearts rather than their appearance? St. Elzear and Blessed Delphina, pray for me.

September 26 Saints Cosmos and Damian (died 303) were twin brothers, born in Arabia, who gained a wide-spread

reputation for practicing medicine and healing without asking for payment. They were dubbed "the silverless" ones, but they succeeded in bringing many into the church in this way. Both were seized and asked to recant their belief in God, but they refused. They were subjected to torture in several horrible ways that, miraculously, did not kill them and so they were beheaded.

Sts. Cosmos and Damian, you gave freely of your medical skills to those who had nothing and your loving care brought many to God. There are many homeless and poor people today who have no access to medical care except through volunteer medical personnel and state agencies. Can I say a prayer each day for the workers who care for these people and look for ways I can help too? Some agencies may need help setting up appointments, and health and suicide hotlines need volunteers. What can I do to help? Sts. Cosmos and Damian, pray for me.

September 27 St. Vincent de Paul (1580-1660) was on board a ship bound for Toulouse, France, where he worked as a tutor, when he was captured by Turkish pirates, brought to Tunis, and sold as a slave. He was able to convert his master to Christianity and returned to France, and for the rest of his life he worked to help slaves along with the poor and abandoned. The

good work was divided between the Sisters of Charity who nursed the sick and cooked for them and the Priests of the Mission who collected food and clothes for the poor. St. Vincent established seminaries and hospitals, persuaded rich women to solicit funds for his missions, and ransomed galley slaves from North Africa. The Vincentians and the Sisters of Charity continue their work today, many through parish churches.

St. Vincent de Paul, the work you started to help the poor goes on today so many years after your death. As God said, "The poor will always be with us," and so we will always need the work your followers do. Do I do as much as I can to help those less fortunate than I or do I turn a blind eye on their needs? When my church has a food drive for the poor, do I donate generously? How can I follow your example of loving charity? St. Vincent, pray for me.

September 28 St. Lorenzo Ruiz and Companions (1600-1637) were a group of several priests and two laymen, Lazaro and Lorenzo, a devout Catholic and father of three, who traveled to Japan from the Philippines. At that time Christians living in Japan were being persecuted and killed or made to leave. St. Lorenzo and his companions were seized and tortured in several especially gruesome ways. St. Lorenzo was tempted to renounce his faith if

his life was spared, but he did not give in to the temptation. He and his companions were hung upside down until he and Lazaro were dead. Then the priests were beheaded. Lorenzo is the first canonized martyr from the Philippines.

St. Lorenzo, you and your companions suffered horribly for your faith. I'm afraid that if I had to submit to the inhumane torture you suffered, I would not be as strong as you. What keeps me from talking about my faith? Is it that I want to be politically correct, or do I fear ridicule. Can I dare to profess my faith loud and clear as you did? Can I resist the temptation to remain safe and silent? St. Lorenzo, pray for me.

September 29 Sts. Michael and Raphael, Archangels are both mentioned in the bible along with the angel Gabriel. On September 29, a basilica near Rome was dedicated to St. Michael the Archangel. In the New Testament, a great battle is described between Michael and his angels and a dragon and his angels. Michael defeats the dragon, Satan, who is cast out from Heaven. *(Revelation 12:7-9)* Michael is merciful and is believed to be close to God and able to intercede powerfully with Him.

St. Raphael the Archangel was sent by God to restore the sight of Tobias the elder and help young Tobias as well. He made possible the marriage of Tobias and Sara whose previous seven bridegrooms had died on their wedding night. He is thought of as a healing angel. *(The Book of Tobias-Old Testament)*

St. Michael the Archangel, you fought with Satan and succeeded in casting him out from Heaven. Please pray for me that I will be successful in recognizing and fighting the devil's temptations so that I can cast him out of my life. St. Raphael the Archangel, you helped Sara and Tobias marry. Today so many couples live together without the benefit of marriage and many marriages end in divorce. Is there anyone I know who is considering a live-in arrangement or a divorce? Can I help them seek God's help in their dilemma without being intrusive? St. Raphael, pray for me.

September 30 St. Jerome (331-420) is remembered not only for his translation of the Bible from the original Hebrew into a Latin version known as the Vulgate but also for his bad temper and sarcastic writings! If this saint, who had a great love for God, felt that anyone was leading others away from God, he didn't hesitate to criticize them soundly. St. Jerome had been an avid student of Latin and Greek but discontinued his classical studies and concentrated on the Bible after he saw Christ

standing before him telling him he was not a true believer. St. Jerome believed that if you did not know the Scriptures, you did not know God.

St. Jerome, you had trouble controlling your temper when you saw others doing something that you felt was counter to what God would want and, at times, you were condemned for your actions. How can I learn from your problems with your temper to control mine so that I can offer suggestions and help in a peaceful way? Instead of losing my temper, can I offer up the prayer "Jesus, mercy" until I feel calm again? St. Jerome, pray for me.

+October Opening Prayer+

As I look at the wonder of this season, the vibrant colors, the feel of approaching coolness, I praise you for the beauty of this world you created, Lord, this wonderful world you made for us to enjoy. *"The heavens proclaim thy wonders, O Lord, and thy faithfulness in the assembly of the saints." Psalm 88:6*

October 1 St. Therese of Lisieux, the Little Flower (1873-1897), is remembered for many things: her great love for Jesus, her patient physical suffering, the many miracles attributed to her, and her declaration that when she left this earth she would spend eternity doing good for others. Her "little" way to the Lord was made up of many sacrifices not least among them offering love to those she disliked. She

248

admitted that it was a trial for her to associate with some of the nuns in her convent, but those were the very women she sought out, befriended, and spent time with, often helping them to feel loved and therefore improving their dispositions.

St. Therese, we all have certain people in our lives whom we would like to avoid. Yet you have shown us it's possible to overcome dislike and show charity to those very people, benefiting everyone involved. How can I be a friend to someone I don't really like? How can I follow your example and go out of my way today to seek out someone who may have need of a friendly word? St. Theresa, Little Flower, pray for me and help me imitate your "little way."

October 2 Guardian Angels. Pope Paul V added this feast day to the Roman calendar in 1615. Isn't it a comforting thought that we are all protected by an angel whose job it is to help us through this life? Different beliefs about guardian angels come to us from various saints. Saint Jerome, for instance, believed that people could drive their guardian angels away with their sins, and Saint Ambrose thought that saints lost their guardian angels to make their struggle to achieve sainthood more difficult. Honorius of Autun, a Christian theologian, gave voice to the most popular belief about these

angels: that the soul of each person possesses its own guardian angel to help him through this life and to lead him to Heaven when life is done.

Guardian Angel, I know that you are nearby protecting me and speeding my prayers to God. I thank you for your care, I pray that my sins never drive you away from me, and I wait for the day when I will see you and you will lead me to Our Father in Heaven.

October 3 St. Mother Theodore Guerin (1798-1856) left her native France and settled in America with the words, "With Jesus we shall have no fear," on her lips. They sustained her through the difficult trip by ship, stagecoach, steamboat, canal boat, and train to Indiana's wooded frontier. She had no money and no English skills and had to work under an overbearing bishop yet she managed to start several Catholic schools; found a new congregation, the Sisters of Providence; and establish a girls' academy now known as St. Mary of the Woods College. She trusted greatly in God's Providence, sure that He would provide all she needed in his own time.

St. Mother Theodore Guerin, through all the trials you experienced in doing God's work, you never lost trust that God would come through for you. You were not impatient, as I often am, for him to do his work, but respected his judgment about when the time would be right for your prayers to be answered. How can I become less impatient and trust that my prayers will be answered in God's time, not mine? How can I remind myself of God's providence, knowing that He will always provide what I need, although perhaps not always what I think I want, for the good of my soul? St. Mother Theodore Guerin, pray for me.

October 4 St Francis of Assisi (1182-1226) was born into a wealthy family and had a rather flighty youth. One day while praying in a decaying chapel, he heard a voice saying, "Repair my church." St. Francis began to physically restore the chapel, only later realizing that the command had a spiritual meaning for him to help restore Christ's church as a whole. He began helping the poor, living and dressing as they did, bearing witness to the gospel of love and poverty that Jesus had preached. Soon other young men joined him and the order, the Friars Minor, had its beginnings. A few years before he died, St. Francis received the stigmata, Christ's wounds, on his hands and feet causing him great physical suffering that he welcomed with joy.

St. Francis of Assisi, you willingly gave up worldly pleasures and lived a life dedicated to helping the poor and building up God's church here on earth. Am I imitating your self-

sacrificing spirit and helping build God's church? Do I volunteer for service in my church? Do my actions and words bring non-believers to God? Do I ever invite anyone to church services or classes? Do I practice self-sacrifice by giving up some pleasure and offering the gift to God? What can I do today to show my love for God and his church? St. Francis of Assisi, pray for me.

October 5 St. Mary Faustina Kowalska (1905-1938) seemed to have a very humdrum exterior life as a member of the Sisters of Our Lady of Mercy working as a cook, porter, and gardener in several of the order's convents. Her interior spiritual life was far different. This saint received revelations from Jesus which she recorded in her diary, revelations that spoke of Christ's mercy for sinners. St. Mary Faustina was given three tasks: reminding people about God's mercy, encouraging veneration of the image of the Divine Mercy with the words, "Jesus, I trust in you," and developing a movement of laypeople and religious who proclaim God's mercy.

St. Mary Faustina Kowalska, your mission on earth was to share God's message of mercy to sinners. Your prayer, "Help me, O Lord, that my tongue may be merciful, so that I should never speak negatively of my neighbor, but have a word of comfort and forgiveness for all," is one I pray for myself.

God sees no differences in his people; He shows mercy to all. Do I accept others as they are? Do I practice forgiveness? As an act of mercy, do I turn my back on gossip and refuse to repeat it? St. Mary Faustina, pray for me.

October 6 St. Bruno (1030-1101) wanted to live a solitary life and, acting on a vision of a secluded place where he could spend his life in communion with God, went there and founded the first order of the Carthusians. He and the members of his community supported themselves by copying manuscripts with great precision and care. Because the Carthusians did not approve of public honors, St. Bruno was never formally canonized, but the pope gave permission to celebrate his feast day and, in 1623, his name was added to the Roman calendar.

St. Bruno, the beautiful manuscripts that you and your followers produced are a lesson in what working carefully and with mindfulness can accomplish. Do I exercise as much care when talking to God as you did in preparing your manuscripts? If I compare each word I speak to God with each deliberate stroke of your pen, will it help me focus all my thoughts on him? Will you pray for me as I try today to make my prayers more focused and mindful?

October 7 Our Lady of the Rosary This feast was established in 1573 by Pope Saint Pius V. The meaning of the word "rosary" is crown of roses, a spiritual bouquet given to the Blessed Mother. St. Dominic and his followers are mainly responsible for the spread and popularity of this prayer and, in fact, the series of five decades of prayers that we say today is called the Dominican Rosary.

Dearest Blessed Mother, you gave us the rosary as a powerful prayer for peace. Knowing that you told us to pray the rosary for peace and aware of the great need for peace in our times, why don't I pray the rosary more often? When can I find a few minutes today to talk to you through this sacred prayer? I will look for the time because I want to grow closer to you, Our Lady of the Rosary.

October 8 St. Pelagia (died c. 461) was a young woman about whom are told many stories. According to them, she was very beautiful and wealthy, and led a wild and wicked life. One day she heard a sermon that somehow touched her heart. Regretting her decadent past, she converted and spent the rest of her days serving God, masquerading as a man and living as a hermit so she would not be a temptation to others. She stands as an example of not allowing our earthly possessions, attributes, or talents lead others into committing sins against God.

St. Pelagia, once you realized that the life you were leading was not pleasing to God and that you were leading others to sin too, you put your past behind you and resolved not to be a temptation to anyone else again. Am I always conscious of my words and my actions so I don't lead others into temptation? Am I sorry for the times I have sinned and caused others to sin too? Is there anything I am doing right now that may lead others away from God? St. Pelagia, pray for me.

October 9 St. Denis (died c. 258) was a bishop of Paris who was so successful in converting people to the faith that he angered the pagans and they had him beheaded. His corpse was thrown into the Seine, but his friends rescued and buried it. Legend has it that after his beheading, his body rose and carried his head a little distance. He is considered one of the "Fourteen Holy Helpers," a group of holy men and women called upon by the faithful for help when the Black Plague swept across Europe. St Denis was asked to cure headaches.

St. Denis, you were sent to convert pagans to the faith and you did your job so well that you were responsible for many conversions. We are all called to bring people to God, through our words and actions; Jesus himself asked us to spread his word. Does what I do and say lead those around me to God, not away from him? Is there anyone I can invite to Mass or some other church activity so they can begin to learn about my faith? St. Denis, pray for me.

October 10 St. Francis Borgia (1510-1572) was the Duke of Gandia and a good Christian. After a failed try to unite Spain and Portugal by arranging a marriage between a prince and a princess and the death of the mother of his eight children, he gave his title to his son and joined the Jesuits. He assumed a humble role doing menial jobs without complaint and, in fact, didn't like it when anyone treated him as if he were still a duke. The story of a duke becoming a Jesuit was widespread and St. Francis' example led many affluent young men to join the order. Eventually he left Spain going to Rome to become Superior General of the Jesuits and helped spread the Society of Jesus in Florida, Peru, and New Spain. He is sometimes called the second founder of the Jesuits because of the changes he brought to the order.

St. Francis Borgia, even though you were a nobleman, you took on the humblest of jobs when you joined the Jesuits. Can I try to imitate you today by doing whatever work that needs to be done, however menial, without complaint? Will you help me develop a humble spirit? St. Francis Borgia, pray for me.

October 11 Blessed Pope John XXIII (1881-1963) honored all people. When he was the Apostolic Delegate to Turkey and Greece in 1935, he saved the lives of thousands of Jewish refugees by issuing them transit visas from the Apostolic Delegation. He was elected Pope in 1958 after the death of Pope Pius XII. Although his time as pope lasted only five years, he became well-known for his work among the imprisoned, the sick, and people of all religious beliefs. Several Protestant sects respected him as a Christian reformer to the point that, at his death, the very anti-Catholic city council in Belfast flew its flag at half-mast to honor him. This pope's great love for all humanity made him one of the most beloved popes of our times among all people, not just the members of his church, and he is lovingly called "the good Pope."

Blessed Pope John XXIII, you reached out to all people, not just the sheep of your flock. The respect you showed to all God's children made you a well-loved man of peace. You have pointed out the way to respect the ways and beliefs of different cultures even though it might be difficult to understand them. Do I follow in your footsteps by not sharing jokes, e-mails, or anything else that is derogatory to another culture or religion? Do I respect others of all colors, races, ethnicities, and religions by my words and my actions? Blessed Pope John XXIII, pray for me.

<>< <>< ><

October 12 St. Seraphin of Montegranaro (1540-1604) worked as a shepherd when he was young using his time in the meadows to pray. When his parents died, he worked for an ill-tempered older brother for a time then left home at age 16 to become a Capuchin friar. He was put in charge of providing food for the poor and, during a famine, ate only a small fraction of his food so he could give the rest away. One time, having run out of food, he picked most of the vegetables from the friars' garden and gave them to the poor. When his superior scolded him, he said that God would provide. The next day, a new crop of vegetables filled the garden.

St Seraphin, your kindness and love for the poor made you a well-loved man. What your story tells me is that I never have to worry about being without if I share what I have with the poor. As you said, "God will provide." What charities are calling to me for help? Can I donate to them on a regular basis, even if I have to sacrifice some pleasure to do so? St. Seraphin, pray for me.

October 13 St. Edward the Confessor (1003-1066) was a well-loved King of England because of his saintly and gentle ways. Before he became king, he was riding and came to the edge of a cliff when his horse stumbled. St. Edward said a prayer to St. Peter vowing that, if he were saved from death, he

would make a pilgrimage to St. Peter's shrine in Rome. The horse righted itself and Edward rode off safely and was called that very day to assume the duties of king. When the people of England heard that he wanted to take the dangerous trip to Rome, they refused to let him go. To keep his vow to St. Peter, in place of the trip, he rebuilt St. Peter's Abbey at Westminster. His reign was a peaceful one; he gave freely to the poor and religious groups and did not impose taxes.

St. Edward, you were a man of peace, wanting only what was best for your people and you believed in keeping your promises. We need people like you working for peace in our world today. We need politicians who keep the promises they make to their constituents and work in a bipartisan way for peace. What can I do to make this come about? Can I hold my representatives to their promises? Can I pray for them that they make decisions that will bring peace? St. Edward, pray for me and for all men and women who hold power in government in all countries.

October 14 Pope St. Callistus I (died c. 222) was put in control of a bank by his master when he was a slave and he lost all the money entrusted to him. He was imprisoned, but his creditors agreed to have him released on the hope that he could

recover their money. Unfortunately, he could not and was sent to work in the mines. The emperor's mistress later asked that all Christian prisoners be released, Callistus among them. The church at that time under Pope Zephyrinus was beset with many heresies. St. Callistus answered the pope's call to help him with theological disputes and, after he died in 219, St. Callistus was named his successor.

St. Callistus, you knew what it is like to try to do a good job only to fail. Somehow you managed to rise from slavery, failure, and imprisonment to become Pope. What an inspiration you are to me! Does failure makes me doubt myself, or do I know that success depends on trusting in God and not giving up? Do I uncomplainingly accept turns in the road that I did not expect or want as a way of accepting God's will? Have there been times in the past when God has led me from a difficult situation? Be with me, St. Callistus, today and every day, through all my endeavors.

October 15 St. Teresa of Jesus (1515-1582) was also known as St. Teresa of Avila. After many years as a Carmelite nun, she realized the order had become lax and undisciplined. She felt called upon to start a reformed order so, despite debilitating illness and bitter opposition, she led a reform

movement in the Carmelites, and started at least 15 monasteries. Besides having natural beauty, she is said to have been intelligent, full of energy, and determined. Due to her writings, in particular *The Interior Castle*, a guide for all people, she was named a doctor of the church, one of the first women to be named.

St. Teresa of Avila, you didn't let physical illness or criticisms from others stand in the way of accomplishing your goals. You knew what you had to do and you went ahead and did it. Why is it that sometimes I have such a hard time finishing what I set out to do? Is it false pride that keeps me from asking for help when I hit a snag or can't see my way around a problem? I can always ask God for help and I know he has put other people in my life to help me along the way too. St. Theresa, pray for me, that I have the humility to admit I cannot always fight my battles by myself.

October 16 St. Margaret Mary Alacoque (1647-1690) loved God from an early age and spent hours in a chapel before the tabernacle that contained the communion host. Her youth was not a happy one. She was sickly and, after her father died, her family had to live with relatives who were not very kind. She became a nun of the Visitation and one day, while she was praying, Jesus appeared and showed her his Sacred Heart. He

told her to tell others about his Sacred Heart and how much He loved them. Over the next 13 months she had many visions of Jesus. He asked her to show her love for him by receiving Communion frequently especially on the first Friday of each month and to spend one hour on Thursdays in a vigil in memory of his agony. For the rest of her life, she spoke about the promises the Sacred Heart made to those who love Jesus.

St. Margaret Mary Alacoque, you were honored by Jesus and you shared that honor by telling everyone of his Sacred Heart that was pierced and continues to be pierced by our sins. Is any sin worth causing Jesus such pain? Can I ask myself that question whenever I feel tempted to do something that will hurt my Savior and Lord? Can I try to go to Mass on every first Friday of the month and spend some time on the preceding Thursday meditating on his Sacred Heart? St. Margaret Mary, pray for me.

October 17 St. Ignatius of Antioch (50-107) is best remembered for the series of seven letters he wrote about the church on a journey from his native Syria to Rome where he was to be fed to the lions in the Circus Maximus. For the most part, his letters urged Christians to be faithful to the church and to avoid heresies. He also begged the Roman Christians not to try to save him for he wanted to offer up his blood to Christ.

St. Ignatius, you were on your way to a terrible death, yet you spent your last weeks writing letters that showed your concern for the church. What selflessness! Will I become more like you if, instead of dwelling on my problems and needs, I try to do something for the church or for someone who is needier than I? Can I perform an act of charity today to start the transformation of my selfishness to selflessness? St. Ignatius, pray for me.

October 18 St. Luke (*1ˢᵗ century*) never saw Jesus in the flesh, but he talked to those who had known and walked beside him and, in his writings, preserved many parables like the stories of the lost sheep and the prodigal son, and the Pharisee and the publican. About the year 50 he joined St. Paul and stayed with him for several years. Then, after a separation, the men met again and St. Luke loyally stayed with St. Paul for both terms of Paul's captivity, not leaving until St. Paul was martyred in 67.

St. Luke, you never saw Jesus, but you learned as much as you could about him by asking questions of his friends. I can't talk to anyone who knew Jesus in the flesh, but I do have many sources for learning about him: my parish priest, bible study groups, books, meditation, and others who love him. Have I taken the time to investigate ways that will teach me more about Jesus? Do I ever read the parables you recorded and meditate on their meaning? St. Luke, pray for me. I want to get to know Jesus more deeply.

October 19 St. Isaac Jogues (1607-1646) was a French Jesuit priest sent to Canada to do missionary work with the Huron Indians. This was not an easy assignment as the Indians blamed the "blackrobes" for any misfortune that occurred. The Mohawks captured and tortured him for over a year during which time he continued to preach to anyone who would listen. He escaped his captors and recuperated in France, but returned to Canada only to be tomahawked and scalped by an Iroquois chief.

St. Isaac Jogues, you suffered so much at the hands of the people you were trying to help, but you never gave up trying to spread God's word. There are many people in the world today who want to inflict terror and pain on others. Do I ever take the time to say a prayer that the hatred harbored in the hearts of those people be replaced by love for God and good will towards all? Do I pray every day that the world might live in peace in my lifetime? St. Isaac Jogues, pray for me.

October 20 St. Paul of the Cross (1694-1775) was inspired by the crucifixion and death of Jesus and wanted to devote his life to telling others about Jesus' love for us, but, as the oldest son in his family, he first had to help his father support his younger siblings. When he was 26, he lived in a church as a hermit and it was there that he wrote a Rule that described how to live a life dedicated to Jesus on the Cross and invited other men to follow this Rule with him. The congregation was called the Passionists because of its dedication to the passion of Jesus. After being ordained a priest, he spent his life traveling and preaching the memory of Christ's passion.

St. Paul of the Cross, you urged people to meditate on Christ's suffering on the cross so they might fully appreciate the sacrifice He made for all of us when he accepted the role of "Savior of the World." Do I take the time to think about the pain and suffering Jesus must have felt? Do I ever think of how my sins hurt him even more than the nails that held him fast to the cross? Help me to allow Christ's passion lead me to be the person He wants me to be. St. Paul of the Cross, pray for me.

October 21 St. Celine (died c. 45) was well past the age for bearing children and probably had given up hopes for having a child when she gave birth to St. Remigius who became the bishop

of Rheims. Shortly after giving birth, she miraculously restored the sight of a hermit who had prophesied three times that she would have a son. Not much else is known about this saint except that she led a holy and prayerful life until her death. She was buried at Lyon but her relics were destroyed in the French Revolution.

St. Celine, after the prophesy of the hermit was fulfilled and you gave birth to a son, you did your best to raise him to know, love, and serve God and you succeeded. He went on to become a very saintly bishop of the Church. Raising children is not an easy job in any generation and it seems as if it gets harder as the world grows farther and farther away from the teaching of Jesus. Are there children in my family who need direction in finding God? Am I following your example and helping them reach that goal? Am I leading a life that shows that loving God and obeying his commands brings fulfillment and peace? St. Celine, pray for me.

October 22 St. Mary Salome (1ˢᵗ century) was one of the holy women who served Jesus during his public life. Mother of St. James the Greater and St. John the Apostle and wife of Zebedee, she was one of the three women named Mary who served Our Lord and was privileged to be with him when He was crucified and placed in the tomb, and then at his resurrection. After the resurrection, St. Mary Salome settled in

Veroli, Italy and spent the rest of her life preaching about Jesus.

St. Mary Salome, your name and that of St. Mary Cleophas are not as well known as the name of the third Mary who was close to Jesus, St. Mary Magdalene. Nevertheless you served and loved him too. You are a wonderful example that it doesn't matter whether our love and work for Jesus is recognized here on earth because God knows all and our reward will come when we join him in Heaven. When I do a good deed, do I look for earthly rewards and recognition? Is it enough for me to know that God is pleased by what I have done? St. Mary Salome, pray for me.

October 23 St. John of Capistrano (1386-1456) was a doer! He joined the Franciscans, was ordained a priest four years later, and became a brilliant and well-loved preacher of the Gospel, founding many Franciscan communities all over Europe. He became known as a peace-broker, settling a dispute within the Franciscan order, helping to reorganize the "Poor Clares," reuniting the Greek and Armenian Churches for a short time, and, at the age of seventy, leading a crusader army of 70,000 men to win the battle for Belgrade against the Turks.

St. John of Capistrano, you used all your abilities to serve

God in many different ways. You were an active representative of Christ on this earth, not waiting for someone else to do what needed to be done. Am I an active participant in the work of my church or do I let others carry the load? Do I know someone who has a need I can fulfill right now in the name of God? Can I try to do some act, however small, each day that will reflect God's love working through me? St. John of Capistrano, pray for me.

October 24 St. Anthony Mary Claret (1807-1870) was called to visit with four criminals who were about to be executed, none of whom had made a confession or expressed sorrow for their sins. The saint pleaded with them to receive the sacraments and, finally, three of them did. The fourth was at the gallows when he asked to confess. This is what St. Anthony Mary Claret was all about---saving souls from spending eternity in the fires of hell. He spent his life preaching and writing about the word of God to achieve that goal and he founded of the Congregation of Missionary Sons of the Immaculate Heart of Mary (Claretians) and the Teaching Sisters of Mary Immaculate.

St. Anthony Mary Claret, you felt you had a duty to try to save as many souls as you could from damnation and so you preached over 2500 sermons, wrote over 150 books, and traveled wherever your mission called you. God has told us over and over in his Holy Word that He wants every one to join him for eternity. Are any of my friends or family members in danger of losing their place in Heaven? What can I do to show them, through example more than words, how much God loves them? St. Anthony Mary Claret, pray for me.

October 25 St. Tabitha (1st century) was a widow who lived in Joppa performing many acts of charity and doing good works. When she died, the disciples called for St. Peter to come to where she was laid out. He told her to arise and she did. This miracle became the source of many conversions to the faith. The story of Tabitha, or Dorcas as she is sometimes called, is told in *Acts of the Apostles, 9: 36-42.*

St. Tabitha, you were a holy person, doing good your whole life and, even when you died and St. Peter called you back from death, the miracle that restored you brought the life of Christianity to many new believers. Am I following your example by doing good works? Is there someone or some organization in need of my help right now? What good can I do today, at home, at work, or during my leisure time? St. Tabitha, pray for me.

October 26 St. Alfred the Great (849-899) would have preferred to enter the religious life, but duty called him to become King of Wessex. For most of his reign his kingdom was under siege from the Danes and he was forced to wage war. This saint was a renowned scholar translating several religious works into Anglo-Saxon; a patron of education, establishing a court school and inviting scholars from different countries to work there; and a great defender of the faith, enabling the church in England to grow.

St. Alfred, you put aside your desire to enter the religious life and answered the call to duty, a duty made very hard because of the wars you had to wage. It is not always easy to do our duty.. Have I ever turned my back on what was evidently my duty whether to a family member or friend or to God? Have I ever made feeble excuses for not doing my duty? How would my life change if I accepted my duty in the future without complaint? St. Alfred the Great, pray for me.

October 27 St. Frumentius (died c. 383) and his brother were on a trip through Arabia when the ship stopped at a port in Ethiopia. The two boys left the ship to sit under a nearby tree when the crew of the ship and some Ethiopians began fighting ending up with all on the ship murdered. When the two young

men were discovered, they were given to the King of Axum as slaves and eventually became trusted members of the king's household. St. Frumentius used his position to spread Christianity in Abyssinia. He baptized the new king, built churches, and brought many people into the church.

St. Frumentius, you turned a situation that began as a tragedy into one that not only ended well for you but brought many people to God showing me that, however bad things seem, something good can happen if you trust in God. When my life seems to be on a downslide, do I throw my hands up in despair or do I turn to God trusting in his mercy and love? Do I live as if I really believe nothing is impossible to those who follow God's word and work on his behalf? St. Frumentius, pray for me.

October 28 St. Jude, Apostle (1ˢᵗ century) is also known as Jude Thaddeus and was related to Jesus by blood. He was one of the 12 apostles, a quiet and humble man who was so filled with the Holy Spirit at Pentecost that he became a missionary to Syria and Mesopotamia, preaching the virtues of simplicity, humility, and prayerfulness. Often pictured with flame of the Holy Spirit touching his head, St. Jude is a very popular saint; many people pray to him for his intervention in hopeless cases, especially for those who are seriously ill.

St. Jude, the virtues you taught are virtues that I need to practice: humility in recognizing that God is behind everything I do; prayerfulness because I can never thank him enough for his gifts; and simplicity because we live in a world where so much emphasis is placed on material things we can get caught up in a frenzy of buying what we really don't need. Am I humble giving praise to God for what he does through me? Do I pray each day in thanksgiving? Am I mercenary, buying just for the sake of buying? St. Jude, pray for me. I want to live the virtues you practiced.

October 29 St. Abraham of Rostov (12th century) was a pagan born in Russia who became deathly ill. "Jesus, heal me," he prayed and he miraculously recovered. Converting to the faith, he was baptized as a Christian, became a monk, and began teaching other pagans in Rostov, Russia, about Jesus. Like many converts, he became a faithful servant of the Lord. Besides building two parish churches and a monastery, he was a great help to the poor.

St. Abraham of Rostov, when you called on Jesus to heal you, He did. You thanked him in tangible ways by spreading his word among the pagans and helping the poor. How do I thank Jesus when He answers my prayers? Is there some tangible way I can show my gratitude for all the blessings I have received? Can I donate some goods or money to an organization that helps the poor or can I perform an anonymous act of mercy? St. Abraham, pray for me.

October 30 Blessed Angelus of Acri (1669-1739) applied for admission to the Capuchins when he was in his teens, but was refused not once, but twice. He was very disappointed at these failures, but, trusting in God, he never gave up on reaching his goals. Finally, in 1690, when he was twenty years old, he was accepted and ordained a priest. When he began preaching, he faced failure again. His first sermons were not very successful or well-received, but he kept trying and practicing and his persistence paid off. He became a famous preacher converting thousands to the faith and performing many miracles.

Blessed Angelus, you never let disappointments stop you from fulfilling your dreams. I want to be like you in that way. When I fail at something, it's hard to pick up the pieces and try again. Do I give in to disappointment and give up on reaching my goal after the first attempt or do I try harder to succeed? Do I trust that God is by my side helping me start over whenever I fail in my first attempt? Do I thank God when success is finally mine, admitting that, without him, there would be no success? Blessed Angelus, pray for me.

October 31 St. Wolfgang (934-994) was one of the three "stars" of the tenth century influencing not only the church but all of civilization. Along with other missionaries, he was sent to evangelize the heathen Magyars who were a threat to the Medieval German Empire until they were converted. He was later named Bishop of Ratisbon, serving as a tutor to several influential persons including the Emperor St. Henry II whose holy life reflects the teachings of St. Wolfgang. He used his position to restore and reform monasteries, promote education, and, like so many of the saints, he was a benefactor to the poor.

St. Wolfgang, you had a great effect on world affairs through your missionary work, through your work as a teacher to Emperor St. Henry II and other historically important persons, and through the reforms you introduced in your diocese. We can all work for peace and make the world a better place. Do I influence others, through my example and my words, to love one another and live in peace? Am I forgiving of the faults of others and humble in asking that they forgive my faults too? Is there someone who needs my forgiveness right now? St. Wolfgang, pray for me.

+November Opening Prayer+

Heavenly Father, we remember all that you have done for us and we give you thanks and praise. *"It is good to give thanks to the Lord, to sing praise to your name, Most High, to proclaim your love in the morning, your faithfulness in the night." Psalm 92:2-3*

November 1 All Saints Day was proclaimed a feast of the church by Pope Gregory IV in 837, and is a celebration of all God's saints, canonized or not. For Catholics it is a day of obligation, a day when they must attend mass. The Church canonizes people who have led holy lives and have performed two miracles, or if they are martyrs, at least one. There are many holy people, however, who have never been canonized, that is recognized here on earth, but who are saints in Heaven.

Don't we all know people in our own lives who have led saintly lives, trusting in God and doing the best they could in whatever circumstances they found themselves? We try to imitate them all and hope to join them one day as Saints Triumphant.

Holy Saints, you are honored this day because you showed the way to God when you were living, and you continue to lead us to his kingdom. By learning about you, I hope to imitate your high moral standards and your charity to others. I want to be like you. Please pray for me that I might be worthy of sainthood in God's eyes.

November 2 All Souls Day

When people we love die, we feel saddened and tears come easily. Jesus cried too when his good friend Lazarus died, but he raised him from the dead. Jesus will also raise us and our loved ones from the dead, not to life on this earth, but to a place we can only dream about, a place at his side in a life that is eternal. The souls in Purgatory, members of the Church Penitent, wait patiently knowing the day will come when God will raise them up.

Holy souls waiting to experience the joy of seeing God, you are being purified so you will be worthy of Heaven. In 2 Machabees 12:46, we are told "it is therefore a holy and wholesome thought to pray for the dead, that they may be loosed from sins." Do I remember to pray every day for the souls in Purgatory, especially for those who have no one to pray for them, and for all my family and friends who have gone before me that they will see God's glory soon? Holy souls, pray for me.

November 3 St. Martin De Porres (1579-1639) was a mulatto, born in Peru of a Spanish knight and a free black woman from Panama. As a youth, he learned medicine from a surgeon-barber, knowledge that came in handy when he was older as, after he became a Dominican brother, he was put in charge of the infirmary. Despite the fact that he faced a great deal of prejudice because he was black, he treated all who were sick regardless of race, color, creed, or station in life. Begging for money and food to care for his charges, he opened a shelter for dogs and cats as well as a hospital and an orphanage.

St. Martin De Porres, you faced prejudice because of the color of your skin, but you continued with the mission you felt God had intended for you. Prejudice is ignorance. Do I look down on any other human beings because they are different from me? Do I treat everyone the same regardless of their color, race, creed, or status in life? Can you pray for me that I might imitate your loving charity to all?

November 4 St. Charles Borromeo (1538-1584) had a speech impediment, but, nevertheless, held many important positions in the church and is considered one of the greatest figures of the Reformation. Despite his prominence, he remained humble and worked hard to reform the church and to bring lapsed Catholic back into the fold. As Archbishop of Milan during the plague and famine of 1576, he borrowed money so he could feed tens of thousands of hungry people every day and stayed in the city helping to care for the sick when he could have left with the city authorities. He founded schools, seminaries, and hospitals and started the Confraternity of Christian Doctrine, an association formed to provide religious education.

St. Charles, you did not let your handicap prevent you from doing the work God sent you to do. You became an important leader in the Church, serving in many capacities, from helping the poor to working with the Pope as a trusted administrator. Am I letting some lack or imagined lack stop me from serving God? Do I believe that God has given me everything I need to do his work or do I find excuses for not answering his call? What one thing can I do today to make this a better world? St. Charles, pray for me.

November 5 Venerable Solanus Casey (1870-1957) had a difficult time with his studies for the priesthood. Once he was ordained a Capuchin, his superiors felt he was weak in knowledge of theology, so he was not allowed to preach or hear confessions, but instead worked as a porter and sacristan. So how did this humble man become one of Detroit's best known priests? People soon discovered that he had the gift of speaking with fire and emotion, and hundreds came to him each week for his blessing and to consult with him, many attributing their cures to him.

Venerable Solanus Casey, studies were hard for you, and your superiors didn't have faith in your ability to instruct or preach. You didn't need recognition from others to use your talents, just quietly went about your business of bringing souls to God. It's easy to lose faith in my abilities when others don't recognize them. How can I imitate you and use the talents I know I possess without waiting for recognition or approval? How can I have confidence in my capabilities and use the talents God has given me without doubt or fear? Venerable Solanus Casey, pray for me.

November 6 St. Nicholas Tavelic and Companions (died 1391) went to the Holy Land to take care of holy sites and look after Christian pilgrims. The four did this work for several years

279

before trying to convert the Muslims to Christianity. After they went to a large Mosque in Jerusalem and spoke about the Muslims accepting Jesus as their Savior, they were imprisoned, beaten, and beheaded. They are among the 158 Franciscans who have been martyred in the Holy Land since 1335, when the order assumed the duties of caring for the holy shrines.

Sharing God's word is one of the ways we show we accept Jesus as our Savior. St. Nicholas Tavelic, you and your companions gave your life trying to teach others about Christ. How do I show I'm a Christian? Do I pray before my meals, even when dining out? Do I read God's word and share what I have learned? Do I attend church regularly and receive the sacraments? Holy saints, pray for me. I want to show that I am a believer of Christ through my love for others.

November 7 St. Didacus (died 1463) went to Rome with fellow Franciscans to celebrate their jubilee. His companion became ill and St. Didacus nursed him back to health. His superiors, noting how effective his care for the sick man was, asked him to stay in Rome and care for the many friars who had become ill while there. St. Didacus stayed for three months; many miraculous cures that occurred during that time are attributed to him. This saint was a lay brother and, because of

his great holiness and success in converting people, was elevated to the position of Guardian of a Franciscan Community in the Canary Islands, a rare position for a lay member. He spent the last remaining years of his life in his native country, Spain.

St. Didacus, your holiness was evident whether you were a leader in the Franciscan Community or an infirmary worker in a convent. One definition for a holy person is one who has absolute adoration and reverence for God Almighty. Your love for God led you to care for others both physically and spiritually. Am I doing anything to nurture those around me by my concern for their physical and spiritual welfare? Do I know someone who could use some care or comfort right now? Can I make the time to offer my help? St. Didacus, pray for me.

November 8 Blessed John Duns Scotus (1265-1308) was a famous Franciscan theologian who taught at Oxford, Cambridge, and the University of Paris. He successfully defended the doctrine of the Immaculate Conception which states that Our Blessed Mother was conceived without original sin. Although this doctrine came into dispute in later years, Pope Pius IX, using the work of Blessed John Scotus, affirmed the Marian doctrine in 1854.

Blessed John Duns Scotus, you believed in the Immaculate Conception of Our Blessed Mother. You carefully prepared your arguments and asked Our Lady for help in presenting them to leaders of the Church. Blessed John, am I prepared as you were to give thoughtful answers to questions about Our Blessed Mother? Do I try to give informed replies instead of shrugging off questions about her and our faith for fear of offending anyone? Blessed John, pray for me.

November 9 St. Theodore Tyro (4th century) joined the Imperial Army of Rome when he was a young man. When the emperor decreed that all Christians had to take part in a pagan ceremony, St. Theodore refused. He was brought before the tribune of his legion and the governor who freed him. His freedom did not last long as he immediately set fire to a pagan temple. A judge offered to spare his life if he would renounce his faith. He answered that he would confess the name of Jesus as long as he had breath. For this declaration, he was burned to death in a furnace.

St. Theodore, you were a brave man, faithful to your beliefs, and for that you were martyred. You were a true soldier of Christ. Am I a good soldier of Christ? Do I always act according to what I believe? Have I ever lacked the courage to speak up when someone has used your name in a joke or as a curse? St. Theodore Tyro, pray for me. I need help to be brave for Christ.

November 10 Pope St. Leo the Great (died 461) was one of the most important popes of the early Church, serving in that position from 440 to 461 during a time of many fierce barbarian invasions on the Roman Empire. He was known as a mediator and peacemaker so eloquent and convincing that he persuaded Attila the Hun to turn back from the gates of Rome by traveling to where Attila and his fierce army were poised to conquer Italy and threatening the barbarian leader with all the powers he held in the name of Peter, the first leader of the Roman church. In another instance, he confronted the Arian Vandal King, Genseric, and successfully prevented him from harming the Roman people even as the king's army plundered the city.

St. Leo, you had the courage to confront men known to be cruel and heartless barbarians without fear, trusting that God was with you. Is there something or someone I fear right now? Are my fears real or imagined? Do I have the courage to confront my fears by putting them in God's hands and working towards eliminating them from my life? Pray for me, St. Leo, that I might have the courage that is born from trusting in God.

November 11 St. Martin of Tours (316-395) converted many nonbelievers to Christianity, tearing down pagan temples and rebuilding churches in their place. By law he had to serve in the army but he refused to take up arms when the Franks and Allemanni invaded the Empire. He told his commanding officer, "Put me at the head of the army without a weapon because I will not draw a sword. I am a soldier of Christ." The most famous story about this saint is of him cutting his cloak in two to cover a poor beggar. His compassion for prisoners was so strong that, in order to have some freed, he agreed to take Communion with a man he had condemned. He regretted this greatly, but an angel appeared to him and told him not to dwell on the past as that is the way to lose one's salvation.

St. Martin of Tours, you made what you felt was a terrible mistake, and it was hard to put it behind you and go forward with your life. But, who hasn't done something that he or she regrets later in life? Am I having trouble letting go of something that happened in the past that I regret? Can I ask forgiveness and get on with my life? God says, "All is forgiven if you repent." If God can forgive me for all the wrong decisions I have made that I repent, then why can't I forgive myself. St. Martin of Tours, pray for me.

November 12 St. Josaphat (1580-1623) worked hard promoting unity of the Roman Catholic and Eastern Orthodox Churches. For over 500 years, the Catholics in Russia had declared themselves independent of the Roman Catholic Church, but, in 1595, some Eastern Orthodox Church leaders wanted to reunite with the Holy See. St. Josaphat succeeded in bringing the churches together for a short time, but those opposed to the union established a non-Roman archbishop and won many people away from the Roman church. As St. Josaphat struggled to bring back unity, enemies entered his church one night and killed him.

St. Josaphat, you preached unity and worked hard to bring it about. Today we still don't have unity among all religions, even among Christians. Is there anything I can do to bring about understanding between people of different faiths? Do I show by my actions that I am a Christian who loves God and wants peace between people of all beliefs? St. Josaphat, pray with me that all peoples unite in their love and praise for one God.

November 13 St. Frances Xavier Cabrini (1850-1917) was refused admittance to a religious community in Italy because her health was so poor but, after working at an

orphanage, she was able to take her vows at a later time. She had a strong desire to work in China as a missionary, but another disappointment was in store for her. She was sent instead to New York to work with Italian immigrants. When St. Frances arrived in New York, there was no house where she could establish an orphanage, so the bishop told her to go back to Italy. Refusing to let difficulties put an end to her mission, she stayed and found the means to open orphanages, schools, and a hospital. She and her companions founded the Missionary Sisters of the Sacred Heart.

St. Frances Xavier Cabrini, you certainly had lots of reasons to be discouraged, but your spirit never allowed you to despair. You accepted God's will for you and became a beacon of hope for many of the poor. Sometimes I don't understand why my prayers are not answered in ways I want them answered. Do I trust that God knows what is best for me? Do I accept his will, as you did, without complaint? Mother Cabrini, pray for me, that I might accept God's plan for my life.

November 14 St. Lawrence O'Toole (1125-1180) was on a trip to England when a madman struck him a blow to his head. Everyone thought he would die, but, to their surprise, St. Lawrence came to and asked for some water. He blessed the

water and, after cleaning his wound with it, the bleeding stopped, and he went on to celebrate Mass. St. Lawrence was the Archbishop of Dublin whose duty was to visit with King Henry II of England for various reasons, once to negotiate peace between the monarch of Ireland and the king after the English had invaded Ireland.

St. Lawrence, you recovered from a wound that should have taken your life. There is no illness or injury that God cannot heal. When we or someone we love needs God's healing hand upon them, prayers can work wonders because God always answers our prayers in a way that is most beneficial to us. Do I pray for my loved ones to recover from illness and, at the same time, trust that God will give them and me courage to face whatever suffering their illnesses bring? St. Lawrence, pray for me.

November 15 St. Albert the Great (1206-1280) was a Dominican priest with an insatiable thirst for knowledge. He was a recognized authority in several of the sciences with many books and other written work to his credit; he was also very knowledgeable about the bible and God. He coupled his immense curiosity for knowledge with a great love for God and believed that science and religion could coexist. Studying the works and ideas of Aristotle, he was the first medieval scholar

to apply those philosophies to Christian thought. He taught in several institutions of higher learning with St. Thomas Aquinas as his most famous student.

St. Albert the Great, you were a scientist but you never lost sight of the fact that God is the source of all matter. In modern times, when science has taken such giant leaps, some scientists overlook the sanctity of human life under the guise of scientific discovery and advancement. Do I respect all human life from conception to death? Do I volunteer to work for organizations that promote life; do I write to my representatives in government about right to life issues; do I support pro-life political candidates? St. Albert the Great, pray for me and for all whose human rights are not recognized.

November 16 St. Margaret of Scotland (died 1093) was living in England when the Normans conquered that country. When her father died, her mother decided to take the family to the continent, but the ship they were on blew off course and landed in Scotland. Malcolm III, king of Scotland, took the family under his protection, fell in love with Margaret, and made her his queen. She was a pious person, an active queen who instigated church reform, invited the Benedictine Monks to establish monasteries in Scotland, visited the sick, and ordered

hostels built for the poor. But there was another side to St. Margaret; she was a very fashion-conscious woman. In addition to her spiritual activities, she also improved the Scottish economy by building closer ties with the European continent through her introduction of European fashions and customs to her court. She was a patron of the arts and education and often advised her husband on government affairs.

St. Margaret, you used your position as queen to build up the church and your country and improve the lives of all around you. What an example you are!! Everyone, men and women alike, can, like you, be the driving force behind changes for the better in the church, in government, and in providing charity to the needy. Do I take an active role in my church? Do I keep abreast of what is going on in government, both local and national, and let my voice be heard to civic leaders? Do I give generously to charities? St. Margaret, pray for me.

November 17 St. Elizabeth of Hungary (1207 -1231) was the daughter of Alexander II, the king of Hungary. When she was four years old she was betrothed to marry a nobleman, Louis of Thuringia. Despite the fact that her husband became king, St. Elizabeth lived a simple life that included doing penance and performing works of charity for her subjects. The couple had three

children and then tragedy stuck: Louis was killed while fighting for the crusades. Elizabeth decided to leave the court and, after making arrangements for her children's care, she renounced the world and became a tertiary of St. Francis. She built a Franciscan hospital and spent the rest of her short life caring for the sick. She was only 24 years old when she died. St. Elizabeth is remembered for welcoming the poor and sick to the palace and visiting them in their homes. One story told about her is that once she was confronted when she was carrying bread to the poor in her cloak and, when the cloak was opened, dozens of red and white roses fell out.

St. Elizabeth, you were following the words of God when He said that whatever we do for one of his, we do for him. How am I helping to care for his people? Do I keep in mind that all I have really belongs to God and He wants me to share it? Am I doing that with a generous spirit? Is there any person or organization that could use my help right now? St. Elizabeth, pray for me. I want to follow God's wishes to love his people as He loves me.

November 18 St. Rose Philippine Duchesne (born 1769) heard a Jesuit speak of his work in the Americas when she was eight years old and decided then that that was her vocation. She joined the Visitation Order when she was 19 and, when

religious communities were outlawed during the French Revolution, spent time as a layperson caring for the sick, establishing a school, and, ignoring the danger, hiding priests from Revolutionaries. St. Rose later joined the Society of the Sacred Heart and, after establishing a convent in Paris, finally realized her dream. America! She set up six establishments that included schools and orphanages west of the Mississippi and worked with Native Americans who gave her the name "Woman Who Prays Always."

St. Rose, you carried a dream in your heart for many years before it came true. You didn't waste your time in dreaming though; while you were waiting you led a very productive life. Am I putting my life on hold while I wait for some dream to come true? Do I tell myself, "When I get that job, I will..... When I lose weight, I will...... When I........?" Am I wasting my time when I could be living a full life as God surely intends me to do? St. Rose, pray for me. I want to use my time fruitfully as you did.

November 19 St. Nerses the Great (4th century) married a princess and they became the parents of a boy who was to become St. Isaac the Great. After St. Nerses' wife died, he served as chamberlain in the court of King Arshak of Armenia

until he was made Catholicos, leader, of the Armenian Church. He devoted a great deal of time to reforming the Church and built hospitals and monasteries. When King Arshak murdered his wife, St. Nerses denounced him and the saint was exiled. St. Nerses returned from exile after the king died, but the succeeding king, Pap, was not much better, and the saint refused to admit him to the church. St. Nerses was poisoned at a royal banquet.

St. Nerses, royalty did not intimidate you. You had job to do and you did it. Censuring two kings could not have been easy, but you willingly accepted the consequences of doing what was right. Am I intimidated by others who may be leading me away from God? Do I "go along" just because I don't want to make waves? Am I afraid of the consequences if I speak against actions or words that offend God? St. Nerses, pray for me. I want to have the courage to do what's right just as you did.

November 20 St. Maxentia of Beauvais (unknown) was an Irish or Scottish woman born into a royal family. She was sought after by a pagan chieftain who wanted to marry her. Wanting to honor her vow of virginity to God, she fled to France and lived as a hermitess on the banks of a river. The chieftain hunted her down and tried to force her to return to

Ireland with him. She refused and he beheaded her at Pont-Sainte-Maxence, where her relics can be found today.

St. Maxentia, you were murdered because you wanted to lead a life of prayer, reflecting on God. You felt your vocation in life was to remain unmarried. Not everyone has to be married or be a religious to serve God; He gives us many choices on how to live our lives. Do I respect the vocation choices of my family and friends? Do I support them in their choices? Can I help anyone now who is making a vocation decision? St. Maxentia, pray for me.

November 21 St. Albert of Louvain (died 1193) was chosen by the church and people to be bishop of Liege, France. Emperor Henry VI, who relied heavily on the bishops to perform many duties for him, deposed St. Albert and appointed someone else to the position. St. Albert traveled to Rome to appeal and Pope Celestine III declared that his appointment was valid. The emperor did not give up easily. He sent a group of his knights to visit St. Albert and they stabbed him to death.

An injustice was done to you, St. Albert, and you took action against it. You took a peaceful way to protest and you were vindicated. Injustice toward anyone, no matter what their position in life, is wrong. Do I see injustices around me? Do I protest or look the other way? Do I know someone who is being treated unfairly? If so, how can I be of help? St. Albert, pray for me.

November 22 Saint Cecilia (died c. 117) promised God that she would live a chaste life as a virgin, but her parents married her to Valerian of Trastevere. Legend says that she told her husband that she had a secret that she would reveal to him if he were baptized. As he was returning from the baptism, he saw her at prayer. At her side was an angel who placed a crown on each of their heads. Because of this vision, Valerian's brother also was baptized and the two men began arranging the burial of martyred Christians. Later, Roman soldiers martyred all three of them.

Saint Cecilia, could it have been your guardian angel who helped convert your husband and his brother to the faith? How often do I think of the angel that God has given each one of us to guide our path on earth and lead us to him when our time on earth is done? Do I ever talk to my angel and ask for advice? Can I give a few moments each day to thank my angel for being here for me? St. Cecilia, pray for me.

November 23 St. Columban (died 615) is considered one of the greatest Irish missionaries. When he was a young man, he was greatly tempted by sins of the flesh and worried about staying chaste. He consulted with a holy woman who advised him to leave his native Ireland and the beautiful Irish women who tempted him so much. He left his home to live in seclusion for thirty years after which he and several companions traveled to Gaul where the church and the government were in a state of disorder. He worked to reform the lax church officials and the low morals of the king's court.

St. Columban, you were tempted by sins of the flesh but you didn't give in to them and you worked to help others overcome their temptations. Have we lost our moral compass today? Television, movies, and many people in the news seem to be saying anything goes. How can I stay chaste in this lax society? How can I help my friends and family live by God's word instead of giving in to the many temptations that surround us? How am I preparing the children in my family to live in this immoral world? St. Columban, pray for me.

November 24 St. Andrew Dung-Lac (died 1839) lived in Vietnam during the reign of Minh-mang, a ruler who hated and persecuted Christians. The king demanded that all Christians stomp on a crucifix to show that they renounced their faith. He also

destroyed churches and religious houses, and decreed that all priests be put to death. St. Andrew was one of 117 martyrs for the church between 1820 and 1862. Despite being the object of persecution for many years and bearing the burden of living in a communist country, many Vietnamese remain faithful to the church.

St. Andrew, the people of your country have suffered for hundreds of years under cruel leaders and from the many wars that have torn the country apart. Yet Christians remain faithful to their church and their God. How strong must their faith be to sustain them through their many trials! How strong is my faith? Do I accept suffering as a path to a stronger faith? Do I offer it up to God, trusting that earthly pain is like a teardrop compared to the ocean of glory that is eternity? St Andrew, pray for me.

November 25 St. Catherine Laboure (1806-1876) walked miles from the farm where she lived in France to attend daily mass when she was a young girl. Later she joined the Sister of the Daughters of Charity of St. Vincent de Paul. At the Motherhouse in Paris, Our Lady appeared to her three times telling her to have a holy medal made with a picture of Mary and the Immaculate Conception stamped on it. Because miracles happened when people wore the medal, it was called the Miraculous Medal. St. Catherine told only her confessor about her visions so no one

knew that she was connected with initiating the Miraculous Medal.

St. Catherine, you obeyed Our Lady so that now we have a beautiful medal to wear that reminds us of how pure Mary was, but you took no credit for your work. It is good to remember Mary's purity especially when we are tempted by impure thoughts. Wearing her medal can be a reminder that she will help us keep our mind and our actions pure. Do I have a miraculous medal? Can I use Mary as my model and imitate her goodness? St. Catherine, pray for me.

November 26 St. Leonard of Port Maurice (1676-1751) was a Franciscan who was a great promoter of devotion to the Blessed Sacrament, the Sacred Heart, the Immaculate Conception, and the Stations of the Cross. During his lifetime, he constructed about five hundred Stations of the Cross throughout Italy, including in the Coliseum. He always thought he would be a missionary to China, but a bleeding ulcer kept him from that work, and instead, after several years spent preaching in Florence, Italy, he was sent as a missionary to Corsica where he brought discipline to the holy orders there.

St Leonard, although you believed your work was in China, it is evident that God thought otherwise. He sent you first to Florence where your preaching was very effective and you were able to bring the way of the cross to many of the faithful and then on a mission to Corsica to bring discipline and order. When I want to do a certain kind of work and I end up doing something else, do I curse God or do I thank him for a new opportunity? Do I welcome new paths with eagerness or with dread? What can I do to embrace life to the fullest no matter where my path leads? St. Leonard, pray for me.

November 27 St. James Intercisus (died 421) was a Christian who renounced his faith when King Yezdigerd I of Persia began persecuting Christians. When the king died, St. James regretted his loss of faith and declared to the new king that he was again a Christian and was sentenced to death. This saint's name, Intercisus, comes from the way he was martyred, his body cut up piece by piece beginning with his fingers.

St. James Intercisus, you renounced your faith probably out of fear, but later recognized what a mistake that had been and courageously announced your return to the faith. We all make mistakes and sin, but your actions show us that it is never too late to repent. Have I gone against God's law in any way, broken any of the commandments? Have I done something to hurt someone? If I have, what I can do to make amends? Pray for me, St. James.

November 28 St. James of the Marches (1391-1476) was a Franciscan priest who dressed in tattered clothes and fasted until he became ill and, it is said, the pope himself told him he had to eat. He preached and performed miracles for 50 years, converting many people to Catholicism as he traveled all over Italy and through 13 central and eastern European countries. Known for his great zeal and energy, he preached every day of his life, fought heretics, promoted unity, and served on delegations throughout Europe. He established several montes pietatis, institutions that lent money on pawned objects to the poor for little or no interest. He is one of the "four pillars" of the Observant Movement within the Franciscans, men who are famous for their preaching.

St. James of the Marches, you didn't waste any time in spreading the Good News. You traveled, from place to place as quickly as you could, rarely taking time to rest, preaching and bringing people to God. Do I take every opportunity presented to me to speak about God? How can I prepare myself so that I am ready to speak up whenever I can? Can I become more familiar with scripture so that I can use bible stories to illustrate a point when appropriate? Pray for me, St. James. I, too, want to share the peace I have found in God's word with others.

November 29 St. Cuthbert Mayne (1544-1577) was born a Protestant in England and was ordained a Protestant minister when he was 19 years old. Because of the dispute between the Pope and King Henry VIII (the king proclaimed himself leader of the Church in England so he could divorce his wife, Katherine of Aragon), it was dangerous to be Catholic at that time in England. St. Cuthbert not only converted to Catholicism, he became a priest. He was able to work in Cornwall for about a year before being condemned for being a priest and saying mass. He was hanged, drawn, and quartered. Pope Paul VI canonized him and he is one of the forty martyrs of England and Wales, a group of martyrs chosen to represent the 300 or more Catholics killed for their faith in England during that period.

St. Cuthbert Mayne, you were a clergyman in another religion when you felt drawn to Catholicism. Following your heart, you converted and then studied to be a priest. I wonder who or what made you leave your religion and embrace the Catholic faith. Do we ever know who our actions and words are influencing? Are my words and actions ones that will influence others for the good or might they lead someone away from God? St. Cuthbert, pray for me.

November 30 St. Andrew, Apostle (1ˢᵗ century) was a fisherman who was so taken with the words of John the Baptist that he became his disciple. He heard St. John call Jesus the Lamb of God and, wanting to discover the meaning of those words, he and a companion followed Jesus one day and told him they wanted to see where He lived. Jesus said, "Follow me." After this, Andrew brought his brother Simon Peter to Jesus and they became his disciples, following him and spreading his word. While St. Andrew was hanging on an x-shaped cross, he preached for two days before his spirit returned to Jesus.

St. Andrew, you were called to something bigger than yourself when you met John the Baptist and Jesus. You willingly gave your life to our Savior. Willingness of spirit is sometimes hard to come by. How willing am I to follow where God leads me? Do I do whatever needs to be done with your spirit of giving? Do I put others' needs before mine? Do I offer my daily work to God? St. Andrew, pray for me.

+December Opening Prayer+

This month, dear Jesus, is the month of your birth when God gave earth His only Son so that one day you could redeem our sins. *"And she brought forth her firstborn son and wrapped him in swaddling clothes and laid him in a manger because there was no room for them in the inn." St. Luke 2:7*

December 1 St. Edmund Campion (1540-1581) accepted a deaconate in the Anglican Church from Queen Elizabeth I even though he was a Catholic. Later, seeing those who were faithful to the Catholic Church embracing martyrdom rather than give up their faith, he resigned his position, went to Rome, and became a Jesuit. Returning to England, he was very successful in encouraging Catholics to be stay loyal to their faith. He was arrested and tortured before being hanged, drawn, and quartered

after which parts of his body were hung on display at the city's four gates to serve as a warning to other Catholics. He is another of the Forty Martyrs of England and Wales.

St. Edmund Campion, you made a mistake in renouncing your Catholic faith, but when you realized what you had done, you took steps to make up for your error. We all make mistakes and we all have regrets. We know that God forgives us our mistakes and so we must forgive ourselves. Do I continue to dwell on my past mistakes or do I forgive myself as God does? What good work can I do to make up for the mistakes I have made? St. Edmund, pray for me.

December 2 St. Bibiana (Vivian) (4th century) and her sister, Demetria, had everything they owned taken from them after their parents were killed because of their Christian beliefs. Then the girls were taken to court. Demetria died while they were at court and Bibiana was placed with a cruel woman who tried to convince her that she should be a prostitute. When Bibiana consistently refused to be talked into leading a life of sin, she was thrown into a mad house for a time and later beaten to death.

St. Bibiana, you went through so much deprivation and suffering, yet you did not give in to your persecutors and you held on to your high moral standards. There are so many temptations today: movies, television, even friends who try to turn me away from God. What temptations call to me today? Can I be as tough as you were so that I do not yield to them however pleasurable they seem? St. Bibiana, pray for me.

December 3 St. Francis Xavier (1506-1552) intended to become a professor but, when he met Ignatius Loyola, joined him in founding the Jesuits. He was one of the first missionaries to the Far East and spent ten years traveling, often walking barefoot, through India and Japan establishing churches wherever he went and baptizing so many people he became too weak to raise his arm. He would ring a bell to bring children to him so he could teach them God's word and ask them to spread the good news. Despite difficult journeys and days filled with hard work, he was a joyful, light-hearted person. When he died he was about to fulfill a lifelong wish to travel to China to do more missionary work.

St. Francis Xavier, you spent many years sharing the Word of God with those who might never have heard of him except for you and you did it with joy and a light heart. Perhaps that is why you were so successful. If I were to share the Word with my family and friends with joy as you did, would I be successful too? Would I be able to touch the hearts of others so that they would turn to Jesus as their savior? St. Francis, pray for me. I want to share my love for Jesus with joy.

December 4 St. John Damascene c. 675- 749) is a Doctor of the Church and one of the last "Fathers of the Church," great Christian writers of the 2nd through 8th centuries, who clarified Christian doctrine and passed it on to future generations. He is most famous for his treatises upholding the use of images as part of a devotional life written after the Byzantine emperor Leo III issued an edict against images and Iconoclasts, those who opposed the use of images, entered churches smashing and defacing statues. His work helped bring an end to the Iconoclast heresy and made it possible for us to use statues and images as a part of our devotional life.

St. John, you weren't afraid to point out that the emperor was wrong to forbid the use of images. I thank you for fighting for something that means a lot to my prayer life. The images of God, Mary, and the saints make it easier for me to focus my mind on my prayers. You also show me that sometimes I may have to rebel against authority if what it tells me to do is not right. How can I get the courage, if I am told to do something unethical or immoral, to refuse with confidence enough to persuade others to take a stand with me? St. John, pray for me.

December 5 St. Crispina (died 304) was a martyr of Africa. She was a wealthy woman, married with several children, who was asked to sacrifice to the gods. When she answered that she believed in only one God and would not bow before idols, her head was shaved and she was mocked publicly. She was threatened with death but she replied that God had given her life and she was willing to die for him with joy. Despite the pleadings of her children, she remained firm in her belief in God and was beheaded while giving thanks to him.

The Old Testament tells us that Abraham prepared to offer up his son Jacob as a sacrifice to God because he had faith that God would take care of Jacob. St. Crispina, you showed that same solid faith that God would take care of your children if you followed his word. You were able to put God first, as we all should do, because of that faith and trust. How strong is my faith and trust in God? Do I really believe with my whole heart that He is walking beside me on my life journey, that I have the strength to do anything with his help? St. Crispina, pray for me. I want to be strong for God.

December 6 St. Nicholas (died c.343) was the son of wealthy parents who died in an epidemic when the saint was very young. St. Nicholas gave his entire inheritance to the poor and dedicated his life to serving God. As Bishop Nicholas, he was well-known for his kindness, generosity, and his love for children. There are many legendary stories told about him saving people from famine, rescuing a kidnapped boy, helping young women who were to be sold into slavery, and caring for the poor. During the persecution of Christians, St. Nicholas was exiled and then thrown into prison. Perhaps because of his love for children and his generosity to others, this saint somehow evolved into the jolly Santa Claus who fulfills the dreams of so many children on Christmas Eve.

St. Nicholas, you were a kind and generous man giving freely of both your belongings and your time, often anonymously. Generosity does not always come easily as it often means putting the needs of others first. Am I selfish, always putting myself and my wishes before those of someone else? Do I share my time and my possessions willingly when they can help someone through a difficult time? What little thing can I do today that will bring a smile to someone's face? St. Nicholas, pray for me.

December 7 St. Ambrose (died 397) was governor of Milan when the Bishop of Milan died. While trying to lead the people to elect a new Bishop peacefully, a cry went up from the crowd that St. Ambrose must be the next Bishop! He refused very adamantly at first, even running away and hiding. When he was finally convinced that this was the road he must take, he was baptized, ordained a priest, and consecrated a Bishop of the Church. He immediately gave away all his worldly goods to the poor and began studying scripture and theology so that he could serve God and the Church in the best way possible.

St Ambrose, you were thrust into a job you did not want, but, when you could not change events, you did everything you could to do the best job possible. We all have things that we must do that we rebel against. Is there a job right now that I am dreading or putting off doing? How can I follow your example and do whatever has to be done in the very best way I can? Pray for me, St. Ambrose, that my trust in God will enable me to tackle, without fear, any challenge that is before me.

December 8 Immaculate Conception of the Virgin Mary

We believe that Our Blessed Virgin Mary was conceived without the stain of original sin. She was filled with grace from God and lived her entire life on earth free from sin. The

Immaculate Conception of Mary was defined as a dogma, a belief that is held by Catholics, by Pope Pius IX on December 8, 1854.

Mary, God chose you to be the mother of his son and He blessed you from the moment of your conception by keeping you free from the stain of sin. God has also blessed me through the sacrament of Baptism that washed away original sin from my soul and by sacrificing the son you bore to atone for my own sins. Yet, I continue to give in to temptation. Do I examine my conscience each night before I go to bed and ask forgiveness for any way that I may have hurt God during the day? Do I show God how grateful I am for his mercy and patience with my faults? Our Blessed Mother, please pray for me, a sinner.

December 9 Saint Juan Diego (1474-1548) was an Aztec Indian convert who walked miles each day to attend mass. One day, on his way to church, he saw a beautiful Aztec lady in the road. He went to the Bishop and told him what he had seen; the Bishop ordered him to bring back a bouquet of Castilian roses from the lady as proof of his vision. The next time Our Lady appeared to St. Juan Diego she gave him the roses which he placed in his cape and carried to the bishop. When St. Juan Diego showed the bishop the roses, the bishop

saw the image of the Virgin of Guadelupe imprinted on the saint's cape. This cloak can be seen in Mexico City at the shrine that was built to Our Lady of Guadelupe.

St. Juan Diego, you were a humble man blessed by the Virgin Mother to carry her message to the people of Mexico. Her choice of you tells me that we are all, poor or rich in money, talent, or wisdom, loved by God and his mother. You walked miles to attend mass while I can attend mass every day of the week with much less difficulty. Do I ever try to attend morning mass during the week or do I limit myself to an hour on the weekend? How am I showing I am thankful for the love showered on me by God and the Blessed Mother? St. Juan Diego, pray for me.

December 10 Pope St. Gregory III (died 741) was attending the funeral of Pope Gregory II when, right in the middle of the funeral procession, the crowd called for him to be the next pope. His first challenge came shortly after he became pope. Emperor Leo III declared that the use of images was forbidden because he claimed it was a form of idolatry. St. Gregory disagreed and called a synod that said strong measures would be taken against anyone who destroyed sacred images. Knowing that the emperor would try to harm St. Gregory, many

people called on him to leave Rome, but he held firm. In retaliation, the emperor tried to kidnap St. Gregory, but the attempt failed when the emperor's ships were destroyed in a storm and his ban on images became meaningless.

Pope St. Gregory III, you knew how important holy images were to the people of your faith and you fought to keep them in churches. I thank you for succeeding. When I look at Jesus on the cross, I see his wounds and I know how much He suffered for me. Looking at images of Mary and the saints is like looking at pictures of loved ones in my family who have died and reminds me of how much I want to be with them someday. Thank you for your work in keeping our holy images safe. Pope St. Gregory III, pray for me.

December 11 Pope St. Damasus I (died 384) ruled as the thirty-seventh pope of the Catholic Church. His papacy came during a time when Christianity was tolerated and many Christians, with the threat of persecution gone, grew lax in their faith. Pope St. Damasus I revered the martyrs who had gone before him and adhered to their standards. He took special care to maintain the catacombs of Rome where many of the martyrs had been buried, designing stone tablets, beautifully carved, that he had erected there to honor those martyrs. He himself

wanted to be buried there but he said he was afraid he would "offend the ashes of the holy ones."

Pope St. Damasus, you kept before you always the spirit of the early church when many gave their lives to follow Christ's teachings. You never forgot the bloody beginnings of our church and what the first martyrs did for us. Do I ever think of those holy people and thank them for their sacrifice? Do I ever thank God that I don't have to suffer as they did to practice my faith? Can I remember to pray for those in the world today who cannot practice their faith freely? Pope St. Damasus, pray for me.

December 12 Our Lady of Guadelupe appeared to a poor native, Juan Diego, on a hill just northwest of Mexico City. She identified herself as the Virgin Mary and asked that a church be built at the site. Before the bishop could agree, he asked for a sign and Our Lady sent dozens of red and white roses through her messenger. She also left her image on Juan Diego's scarf, a piece of cloth that has not deteriorated over hundreds of years. The shrine that was build at the site of her apparition has become the most popular Marian shrine in the world and many thousands of miracles have taken place there.

Our Lady of Guadelupe, your appearance to Juan Diego

began the conversion of Mexico bringing many people to the faith. You are the mother of us all. You love us and bring our cares to your son, Jesus. Dear Mother Mary, I love you in return and I thank you for all your many favors. Pray for me and for our world that we may follow your lead and love all our brothers and sisters wherever they might be.

December 13 St. Lucy (c.283-c.304) walked to the little church of Saint Agatha in Rome when she was very young and prayed for her mother who was ill. St. Agatha appeared to the little girl and promised that her mother would get well and added that Lucy would die a martyr for Christ. Both parts of the prophesy came true. Lucy's mother did get well and when Lucy grew up, she became a nun which angered the Roman who wanted to marry her. He told the authorities of her faith and they put her to death.

St. Lucy, you believed that God would answer your prayers through St. Agatha and He did. You also believed that you would die for your faith but that didn't stop you from refusing an offer of marriage and becoming a nun, a path that was sure to lead to martyrdom. Do I understand, as you did, that life on this earth is fleeting and just a preparation for where I will spend eternity? Am I following a path that will lead me to God? Am I doing everything I can to make sure I will spend eternity in heaven? St. Lucy, pray for me.

December 14 St. John of the Cross (1542-1591) was left homeless when his father died and the destitute family wandered looking for work. When he was 14, he began working in a hospital caring for people who suffered from incurable diseases and madness. He became a Carmelite and, obeying a request from St. Theresa of Avila, set out to reform that order. This so angered some Carmelites that they kidnapped St. John, locked him in a cell, and beat him. He managed to escape and spent the rest of his life writing and sharing his vision of God's love.

St. John of the Cross, your life was hard but you did not become bitter even against your fellow monks who turned against you. You looked to God instead and wrote books that give advice on how to grow in love for God and how to pray. When life deals me a blow, do I turn to or against God? Do I use trials and troubles to grow in my faith as you did? Do I follow the example of Jesus and practice forgiveness of those who wish me harm? St. John of the Cross, pray for me.

December 15 St. Mary Di Rosa (died 1885) always tackled jobs others thought she couldn't do. She supervised a workhouse and opened a boardinghouse for poor girls, helped organize a school for the deaf, and served as superior to the Handmaids of Charity who worked in hospitals. Then war came to Italy and she found herself in the middle of that conflict going out to the battlefield to give comfort to the wounded and working in a military hospital. One night she heard pounding on the door of the hospital and knew it was soldiers there for no good purpose. Even though the only people in the hospital were the wounded and a handful of nuns, St. Mary Di Rosa opened the door and held up a crucifix. Shamed perhaps by her courage and faith, the soldiers went away.

St. Mary Di Rosa, you were not afraid to tackle anything if it would help someone. Whenever you saw a need, you jumped in to do whatever it took to fill that need. You relied on God as you did his work on earth, whether it was helping the poor or facing hostile soldiers. How often have I noticed that someone needed something and turned my back? Have I lost an opportunity to do some good because I was afraid? The next time there is a chance for me to help someone, will I do what I can or will I make excuses? St. Mary Di Rosa, pray for me.

December 16 Blessed Honoratus Kozminski (1825-1916) was falsely accused of being part of a rebellious conspiracy and imprisoned for a year in Warsaw. He became a Capuchin monk and worked as guardian in a Warsaw friary. In 1864 after a failed revolt against the Czar Alexander III, religious orders in Poland were suppressed and the Capuchins were expelled from the city. While in exile, Blessed Honoratus founded 26 congregations that operated independently but later, against his wishes, bishops reorganized them under their authority. Although he did not agree with the bishops, he advised the men and women of the congregations to obey their wishes.

Blessed Honoratus, you had many instances in your life when authorities changed your life. You accepted that you could not change things and you did your best under all circumstances. Your life reminds me of the prayer of St. Francis: "God grant me the serenity to accept the things I cannot change, courage to change the things I can, and the wisdom to know the difference." Do I pray that prayer often enough, and do I live by it? Blessed Honoratus, pray for me.

December 17 St. John of Matha (1160-1213) and St. Felix of Valois founded the Order of the Holy Trinity to travel

to Africa and buy back people captured during the crusades or on the seas. The members of the order also cared for those captives who were too sick or old to travel back with them. On one trip, St. John was attacked in Morocco and left for dead, but he survived and continued on with his ministry. Another time, just as his ship was ready to sail, the Moors removed the rudder and sails. St. John ordered the crew to begin rowing. Then, as he tied his coat to the mast and prayed for God's help, a wind sprang up and the tiny sail carried them to Ostia, the port of Rome.

God can do anything, can't He? He can help the injured and dying, He can make a ship navigate with just a tiny sail, and He can answer our prayers if we just ask. If I really believe that God created the world from nothing, how can I doubt that He can do anything I ask of him? Do I believe that God always answers my prayer even if the answer is not one I would have chosen? Do I thank God for challenges as well as blessings? Is there an area in my life right now that I need to entrust to God? St. John, pray for me.

December 18 Blessed Anthony Grassi (1592-1671) was struck by lightning when he was a young priest praying at the shrine of Our Lady of Loreto. The electrical charge threw him

down some stairs and partially paralyzed him, even scorching his undergarments. He was given the last rites, but he recovered. Afterwards he said that, once you feel you are close to death, you realize that nothing in this world is important. Blessed Anthony Grassi lived his life serenely, never getting ruffled or upset and, because of this marvelous trait, he was greatly sought after for advice and spiritual counseling.

Blessed Anthony Grassi, your near-death taught you that the things of this world do not last and are unimportant when compared to eternity and heaven. You were able to live your life serenely, not getting upset over mishaps or misfortune. How can I live a more serene life? Do I take a minute to call on "Jesus, Mary, and Joseph," when my serenity seems threatened by some event or person? Do I turn the upset over to God, trusting that He will always take care of me? Blessed Anthony Grassi, pray for me; I would like my life to be more peaceful.

December 19 Blessed Pope Urban V (1310-1370) was pope at the time when the papacy was located in Avignon, France, instead of in Rome. Pope Urban moved the papacy back to Rome but only for a short time. Two important events occurred during this brief Roman stay: Charles IV of Germany brought his empress to be crowned by the Pope and agreed to

respect the church in his country and Pope Urban welcomed the Byzantine emperor back to the Catholic Church. Unfortunately the Pope was unable to unite the Eastern and Western churches and they remained divided. When the Anglo-French War broke out, Pope Urban returned to Avignon where he felt he might be useful in seeking peace.

Blessed Pope Urban, you were disappointed when you failed to restore the papacy to Rome and couldn't unite the Eastern and Western churches. Yet you continued with your work of restoring and reforming churches and monasteries and creating universities. When I am disappointed, do I give up or get on with whatever needs to be done? Do I trust that God works hand in hand with me in my struggles? Do I sometimes throw up my hands and give in to despair or do I place my trust in God knowing He will get me through anything no matter how hard it seems? Blessed Pope Urban, pray for me.

December 20 St. Dominic of Silos (1000-1073) learned to love solitude as a young boy when he cared for his father's sheep. He became a Benedictine monk and, while serving as prior of a monastery, he had an argument with the King of Navarre over a piece of land belonging to the monastery that the king wanted. He was exiled to the King of Castille who

made St. Dominic abbot of a monastery that was in very poor condition, physically and spiritually. St. Dominic repaired the buildings and reformed the monastic life there, turning the monastery into one of the most famous centers of learning and liturgy in Spain.

St. Dominic, you accepted the challenge given you by the King of Castille and completely turned around the decaying monastery, both physically and spiritually. My body and my soul have been entrusted to me by God and I must take the best care of them that I can. Am I doing that? What in my spiritual and physical life is a challenge to me right now? Is there anything I can do today to improve my physical and spiritual health? St. Dominic, pray for me.

December 21 St. Peter Canisius (1521-1597) was a kind man adhering to the Jesuit policy of never using harshness to get across a point. He once had a worker who was disliked by everyone around him. St. Peter told him gently and honestly how he might overcome his pride and think less of himself by working and praying harder. To bolster the man's morale, he also asked him for advice and helped the man become less antagonistic. St. Peter wrote several catechisms for different ages and many letters of advice, established universities and

seminaries, implemented decrees of the Council of Trent, led the counter-reformation in Germany, and was an eloquent preacher and successful mediator. He is one of the 33 Doctors of the Church.

St. Peter Canisius, your life was full from morning to night yet you took the time to help another person, talking to him honestly but kindly about his faults. Am I honest with myself about something I have done or am about to do? Is there a friend or relative with whom I need to speak honestly about a concern of mine? Am I forgiving of myself and others when we cannot admit to mistakes we've made? St. Peter Canisius, pray for me.

December 22 Blessed Jacopone da Todi (1230-1306) insisted his wife attend an event that ended in her death as the balcony where she was seated collapsed. Blaming himself, this wealthy lawyer gave up his possessions and began doing penance. His law partners called him "Crazy Jim," a name that caused the Franciscans to refuse his application to join them until he wrote a beautiful poem proving his sanity. Upset because the Pope did not approve of a group of Franciscans who wanted to live in strict poverty, he protested against him. He was excommunicated and imprisoned for five years before

receiving absolution and his freedom. He is considered one of the greatest poets of the middle ages, and is the author of the Stabat Mater.

Blessed Jacopone, you spent your whole life trying to make up for your wife's death which you thought was your fault. Even though people called you crazy for doing so much penance, you continued on with what you felt you had to do. Am I dependent on the approval of others or do I do what I know is right no matter what anyone says to me? Can I find a way to express my failures, my successes, and my love of God in some beautiful way as you did with your poems? St. Jacopone, pray for me.

December 23 St. John of Kanty (1390-1473) was a professor at the University of Krakow when he was unjustly accused of some offense and demoted to the position of parish priest. He was nervous and afraid of his new responsibility and his parishioners were upset that their new pastor was a man who was disgraced. He determined that he would do his best in this lowly position, but it took him many years to win the people's hearts which he did through his kindness, humility, and generosity. He ate sparingly and wore shabby clothes, giving most of what he had to the poor. In later years, he was

exonerated and returned to his teaching position.

St. John of Kanty, you were nervous about the new position you were given that was so different from university teaching, but you didn't let fear stop you from doing your best. Is there a challenge in my life that I am not accepting because I am afraid? Do I welcome new challenges as opportunities even when I feel anxious or nervous? Do I remember to ask for God's help and direction before starting any new venture? What help will I ask of him today? St. John, pray for me.

December 24 St. Emiliana (6th century) dedicated herself to God, along with her sister Trasilla, when she was very young. The sisters, both aunts of St. Gregory the Great, spent many years praying and fasting. One day, one of their dead ancestors appeared to Trasilla asking her to come with him to her "abode of glory." She died soon after and then appeared to St. Emiliana asking her to join her in heaven. St. Emiliana fell ill and died a few days later.

St. Emiliana, you and your sister spent your whole lives dedicated to God. You were very single-minded in your love for him and were ready and happy to go to him when He called. None of us here on earth know when we will be called to leave this life. Will I be ready when it is my time? Will I be able to tell

God that I gave him my best while on earth? When He asks me what I have done to help his people, what will I answer? St. Emiliana, pray for me.

December 25 Birth of Jesus Christ "And Joseph also went from Galilee out of the town of Nazareth into Judea to the town of David, which is called Bethlehem, because he was of the house and family of David, to register together with Mary his espoused wife who was with child. And it came to pass while they were there that the days for her to be delivered were fulfilled. And she brought forth her firstborn son and wrapped him in swaddling clothes and laid him in a manger because there was no room for them in the inn." St. Luke 2:4-7.

What a gift you gave to us, God, in that humble manger! How can I ever thank you? How can I thank Jesus for his willingness to come to earth and die for my sins? How can I thank Our Blessed Virgin for accepting the hardships that went along with following your will? How can I thank St. Joseph for his steadfastness in caring for his wife and child? Whatever thanks I offer can never be enough, but I can love you with my whole heart and soul until someday I see you and thank you face to face.

December 26 St. Stephen (died c. 35) was one of the first seven permanent deacons of the church ordained by the apostles and he was the first Christian martyr. He preached, taught, and helped care for the poor in the Christian community. He also liked to publicly debate the life and teaching of Jesus and was critical of the Jews. He said they were like their ancestors who had rejected the prophets foretelling the birth of Jesus as well as Jesus himself. Accused of blasphemy, St. Stephen was stoned to death, but, before he died, he had a vision of Jesus standing at the right hand of God and he asked God to forgive his enemies.

St. Stephen, you spent your life working for the church and were not afraid to speak the truth about Jesus. So often, in modern times, we focus on "political correctness" and don't speak of Jesus because we don't want to offend anyone. Am I afraid to give witness to my faith, the love I have for Jesus, and the love He has for me and the whole world? When have I ignored an opportunity to speak his name? St. Stephen, pray for me.

December 27 St. John, Apostle (first century) was one of the first apostles chosen by Jesus along with his brother James, and he traveled all over with him becoming known as

the beloved disciple. St. John is the only apostle who did not desert Jesus as He was crucified. As He was dying, Jesus entrusted his mother to John who took Our Lady into his home. He was the first to reach the tomb when news of the resurrection came and he was the first to recognize Jesus at the lake of Tiberius. He preached over and over that the most important thing to learn is that "God is Love."

St. John the Apostle, you were privileged to know Jesus in a close relationship and to be entrusted with his mother after He rose to heaven. You loved him and stayed by his side through good times and bad. Life gets so busy that, when everything is going smoothly, I sometimes forget to take time for God. Then, in times of need, I turn to him. Do I pray only when I need help or do I pray to God each day, in good or bad times? Do I thank him for all He has given me? Morning, noon, or night, He waits to hear my voice. St. John, pray for me.

December 28 Feast of the Holy Innocents (first century)

King Herod was a brutal man. When three wise men arrived from the east asking for directions to find the baby who was to be the "King of the Jews," Herod asked them to return and tell him where they found the child. The Magi, warned by an angel, returned home by another route. Herod, fearing he would lose his throne, decided to kill all baby boys under the age of two, unaware that Joseph, having been warned by an angel, had taken Mary and Jesus and fled to Egypt. These martyred babies are the Holy Innocents, babies who gave their lives in place of Jesus.

Holy Innocents, the horror of your slaughter tells us so much about the violent state of the world at the time of Jesus' birth. Yet today we still see violence all around us, testaments of man's inhumanity to man. Am I ever the source of cruelty to another human being? If I see someone suffering because of cruel actions, do I help them? Do I work and pray for laws that show respect for human life? Do I vote for leaders who respect all life? Holy Innocents, I pray alongside of you who gave your lives in place of Jesus that our world may become the place God wants it to be, a haven of safety and love for all God's children, born and unborn.

December 29 St. Thomas Becket (1118-1170) and King Henry II of England were such good friends that the king named St. Thomas Archbishop of Canterbury assuming that the priest would go along with Henry's wish to have power over the affairs of the church in his kingdom. St. Thomas resisted the king's wishes and had to seek refuge in a monastery for six

years. When he and Henry reconciled, he returned to England and assumed his duties but continued to uphold the belief that the Pope was a higher church authority than the king. King Henry's knights killed St. Thomas in Canterbury Cathedral, a murder that shocked the world.

St. Thomas, you would not allow anyone, even the King of England, to assume the authority that belonged to God's emissary, the Pope. You sacrificed your great friendship with King Henry, your honored position, and finally your life to defend your belief. Am I resolute in my beliefs? Am I even sure of what I believe? Is there a discussion or study group at my church that might help me clarify the church's teachings and my acceptance of them? St. Thomas, pray for me.

December 30 St. Anysia (died 304) was a wealthy Greek woman, a Christian, who used her riches to help the poor. At that time, Christians were being persecuted and attending mass was forbidden. One day, as St. Anysia walked to meet with other Christians, a guard pulled her over and asked where she was going. As she made the sign of the cross on her forehead, he told her that she had to go with him to worship the sun. Refusing to go to the pagan ceremony, she struggled to be set free. The guard pulled out his sword and ran it through her.

After the persecution ended, fellow Christians built a church over the spot where St. Anysia gave her life for Christ.

St. Anysia, you were persecuted for believing in Christ and following in his path. I am blessed to have been born in a country where I am free to worship as I wish. This is not true in so many countries, even to this day. Do I remember to offer my prayers for those in countries where religious freedom is denied? Do I pray for the leaders of those countries that Jesus might enter their hearts and make them see the error of their ways? St. Anysia, pray for me and for all who are denied freedom of worship as well as for enlightenment for their leaders.

December 31 St. Melania the Younger (383-432) knew from an early age she wanted to devote her life to God, but her family made her marry when she was just fourteen. Her desire to serve God never left her and, after the two children she bore died in infancy, her husband and her widowed mother became convinced that they too should spend their lives praying and doing God's work on earth. They gave up their fortunes, freed their slaves, and gave everything they had to the poor. Later, after they had fled to Africa escaping the Goths, St. Melania founded two monasteries, one for men and one for women.

St. Melania, your persistent piety and prayers encouraged your husband, mother, and all you met to turn to God. You taught God's message by example. Does the example I set convince those around me to draw closer to God and to follow his will? Do I persistently pray or does my prayer life sometimes get lost in the busyness of my everyday life? When can I set aside some time each day to pray for the conversion of sinners no matter how rushed and busy I am? St. Melania, pray for me.

Meet Mary A. Lombardo

Mary A. Lombardo has worn many hats in her professional life. Now retired, she has been an educator, union organizer and negotiator, newspaper editor, mediator, and writer. She is the author of eight books for educators including *Mastering Math through Magic, Poetry and Pop-ups*, and *Rhymes, Writing, and Role-Play*. A long-time student of the Bible and a life-time Catholic, her interest in learning about the lives of the saints prompted her to compile the short anecdotes and meditations that make up this book.

She and her husband live in Albuquerque, New Mexico, close to their three grown children and one well-loved grandchild, Joshua.